EXPERT COMPANIONS

AT HOME

SKILLS AND TIPS

EXPERT COMPANIONS

AT HOME

SKILLS AND TIPS

A GUIDE TO
MODERN LIVING

WELDONOWEN
PUBLISHING

CONTENTS

SAVING ENERGY AND WATER

There are many ways to conserve energy and water, and a lot of these measures are a matter of common sense. You'll also be saving money and protecting the environment.

Appliances

Low energy rating In many countries appliances are rated according to their energy consumption, making it easier to choose energy-efficient ones. Look for the international Energy Star logo.

USING APPLIANCES EFFICIENTLY

Small appliances Use a kettle rather than a saucepan to boil water, or a toaster instead of the griller.

Cooktop Match big pots to big burners so you cook more efficiently, and use only as much water as you need to boil or steam.

All appliances Turn all but the fridge off at the wall when they are not in use. Television sets, computers, DVD players and microwave ovens all use power even when in standby mode.

IN THE KITCHEN

Oven Bake more than one item at a time. Use the oven light to check on a cake's progress and only open the door when you think it's ready for the skewer test.

Bar fridge If you live alone in a small apartment in a cold climate, use a bar fridge rather than a family-sized fridge/freezer.

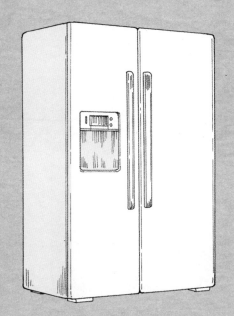

Fridge
* Locate it away from the oven.
* Keep the coils at the back dust-free.
* Check the seals around the doors, and repair them if necessary.
* Only open the door to fetch something – don't hold the door open while browsing.
* When you go on a long holiday, turn off the fridge. Prevent mildew by leaving the door open.

Hot water by the pot Until the 19th century, water was generally heated on top of a wood- or coal-fuelled stove.

SOLAR HOT WATER HEATERS

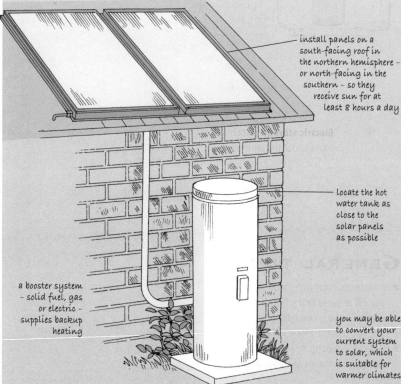

install panels on a south-facing roof in the northern hemisphere – or north-facing in the southern – so they receive sun for at least 8 hours a day

locate the hot water tank as close to the solar panels as possible

a booster system – solid fuel, gas or electric – supplies backup heating

you may be able to convert your current system to solar, which is suitable for warmer climates

ELECTRIC HOT WATER HEATERS

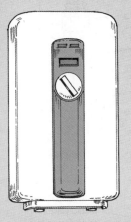

Instantaneous water heaters

This type supplies hot water only when you need it, so you don't waste money keeping water in a storage tank at a certain temperature.

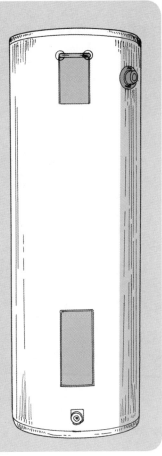

Electric storage water heaters These produce about the same amount of greenhouse gases as the average-sized car.

GENERAL TIPS

* Insulate your hot water heater and locate it as close to the house as possible – the shorter distance the water travels, the less it will cost you.
* Replace an electricity-powered hot water heater with a gas, solar or heat pump one.

* Always turn off the hot water when you go on holidays.
* Lower the water temperature to 50°C.
* Think about installing a heat pump system, which extracts heat from the atmosphere. It's more expensive to install but much cheaper to run.

SOLAR POWER

Harness the sun Although solar power is expensive to install, the sun's energy is a free, clean and renewable source of power with no greenhouse gas emissions. It can also help make your household self-sufficient.

A SIMPLE PRINCIPLE

Early attempts at solar power By the turn of the 19th century more than 1000 solar panels had been installed in Californian homes in the United States.

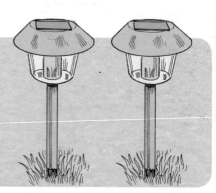

OTHER APPLICATIONS

Solar garden lamp Featuring a photo-voltaic panel on the top, an LED (light-emitting diodes) lamp and a rechargeable battery, this lamp emits enough light to illuminate a garden path.

DOMESTIC SOLAR SYSTEMS

Lower costs Photovoltaic cells in the solar panels convert the sun's energy to electricity. Depending on your climate and the capacity of your system, you could send back power to the main grid, and the lower energy costs will pay for the installation in a few years.

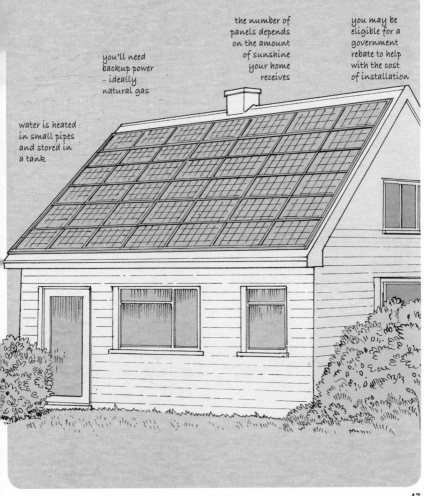

you'll need backup power – ideally natural gas

the number of panels depends on the amount of sunshine your home receives

you may be eligible for a government rebate to help with the cost of installation

water is heated in small pipes and stored in a tank

INSULATION

Reducing heating and cooling costs Insulating both the ceiling
and walls will retain heat in the cooler months but exclude it in summer,
and may also save you up to 50% in heating and cooling costs.

TYPES OF INSULATION

Reflective insulation This
sheeting material comprises layers
of aluminium foil and plastic or
paper laminated together. When
stapled to the bottom of the roof
rafters or laid over existing ceiling
insulation, it reflects heat.

Natural renewable materials
These include hay bales, sheep's
wool, cellulose fibre and hemp.

Rigid insulation Lightweight
insulated boards are made
from layers of plasterboard and
polystyrene or polyurethane.

Rolls and batts Used to insulate ceilings, batts
are made from materials such as fibreglass,
polyester and rock-wool, a type of volcanic rock.

OTHER INSULATION IDEAS

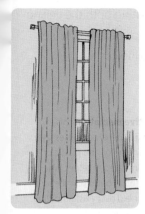

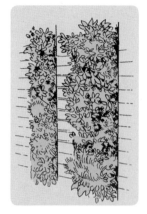

Windows In a cold climate, install double glazing and hang curtains with a thermal lining that can be removed in the warmer months. Draught-proof around all windows.

Entry doors Install weather strips at the bottom of all entry doors and draught-proof the frames using foam strips, permanent mouldings or caulking products.

Vertical garden If you live in a hot climate, plant a vertical garden on a sun-exposed wall.

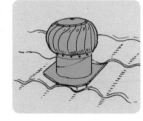

Roof vents Keep bulk insulation dry by installing a few roof vents – they prevent moisture build-up in the ceiling cavity.

Thermal mass In a cold climate, construct a new house with building materials that are slow to heat up and cool – for example, consider stone or brick.

SAVING WATER

Water-wise measures If you follow these water-saving tips, not only will you reduce your water bill, but you will also save on the cost of heating water, which can be more than a quarter of your power bill.

HOUSE TAPS

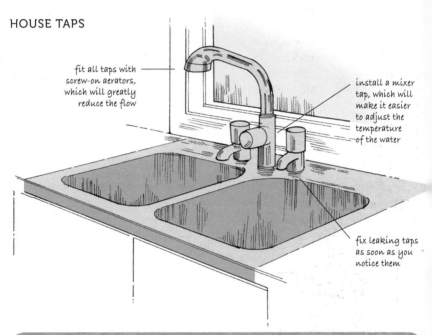

fit all taps with screw-on aerators, which will greatly reduce the flow

install a mixer tap, which will make it easier to adjust the temperature of the water

fix leaking taps as soon as you notice them

CHECKING FOR A LEAK

1 Turn off all the taps in the house and garden.

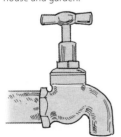

2 Record the reading on the water meter.

3 Check the meter a few hours later. If the reading is higher, there's a leak.

THE BATHROOM

Shower

* Take shorter showers.
* Install an energy-efficient shower rose.
* While the water heats up, use a bucket to catch the cold water, then use it on your plants.

Toilet

Install a dual-flush toilet and use the half-flush as much as possible. If you don't have a dual-flush toilet, place a 2-litre soft-drink bottle full of water in the cistern. It will save 2 litres per flush.

Bath

If you must have a bath, make it only deep enough to cover your body. Make sure you monitor the temperature so you don't have to add lots of cold water to cool it down.

IN THE GARDEN

choose plants that are native to your local area

plant drought-tolerant plants

wash the car with a bucket rather than a hose

cut down on the amount of lawn

install a drip irrigation system and water deeply and less often

make a 'moat' around each shrub and tree so rainwater will soak into their roots

install a
rainwater
tank

conserve water
by mulching
garden beds

dig in lots of
organic matter,
such as compost
and some aged
animal manure

do not hose
down the paths

water in the
early morning
or late evening

Harvesting water

Rainwater tanks You can choose from a range of types, from traditional galvanised iron tanks to plastic ones in a huge range of shapes and sizes, but first check with your local government authority about any regulations.

TYPES OF TANKS

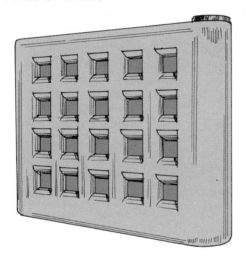

Water wall Large but relatively thin tanks can be used as fences or screens in narrow spaces.

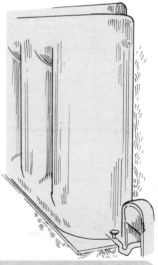

Slimline polythene tank
Suitable for a narrow side passage on the cool side of the house, it should be sited near a downpipe.

First flush You'll need a first flush system to divert the first 5–10 litres of dirty water into the garden.

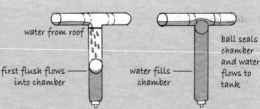

water from roof

first flush flows into chamber

water fills chamber

ball seals chamber and water flows to tank

Galvanised corrugated iron tank Suitable for farms and large gardens, the traditional tank on a stand supplies water through a gravity feed or a wind-powered water pump.

GENERAL TIPS

* The size and type of tank you install should suit the purpose – for example, will you be using rainwater on the garden only, or for the whole household? – and also the amount of space you have available.
* Multiply the roof area by the local annual rainfall to work out how much water you can collect each year – for example, with a roof area of 100 m² and an annual rainfall of 500 mm, you'll collect 50,000 litres a year.
* Fit mesh screens to all inlets and outlets to keep out vermin and insects.
* An electric pump, while not neccessary, will increase the water pressure.

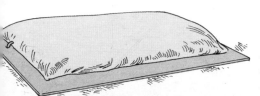

Bladder tanks The advantage of these is that they sit under decking, completely out of sight – ideal for courtyard gardens.

Roofing material Collecting water from the roof means you must use non-toxic roofing materials that won't contaminate the water – for example, ceramic tiles, rather than roofing iron painted with lead paint.

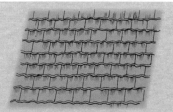

Grey Water

What is grey water? Waste water from the bath, shower, washing machine, dishwasher and sinks can be either used on the garden or filtered for reuse, such as washing clothes or flushing the toilet.

RECYCLING WATER

By hand You can collect bath and shower water in a bucket but you will need to add it to a tank attached to an in-ground irrigation system so it can be filtered before being used on the garden.

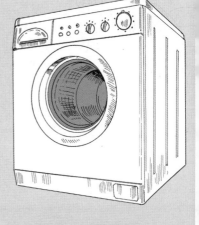

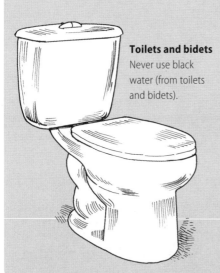

Toilets and bidets Never use black water (from toilets and bidets).

Washing machine If you use waste water from the washing machine, launder only with biodegradable detergents and use only the final rinse water from the washing machine. Never use water from washing nappies.

USING GREY WATER ON THE GARDEN

Warning Don't use grey water from the kitchen sink in case it contains grease and food debris, and never use grey water on vegetables and herbs. Finally, do not store grey water, as the accumulation of bacteria and other micro-organisms can result in a health hazard.

GENERAL TIPS

* Check first with your local government authority to find out if using waste water is permitted in your area. You may be entitled to a rebate.
* Employ a qualified plumber to install a water diverter that will direct waste water to an irrigation system.

* Clean the system regularly and have it serviced by a professional in accordance with the manufacturer's guidelines.
* You'll need to check the sodium levels in your soil and correct the imbalance if necessary.

REED BEDS

Natural filter Basically, a reed bed is a treatment pool containing reeds, such as bullrushes and water mint, growing in a bed of gravel and/or sand. The reeds emit oxygen, which helps to purify the water.

SIDE VIEW

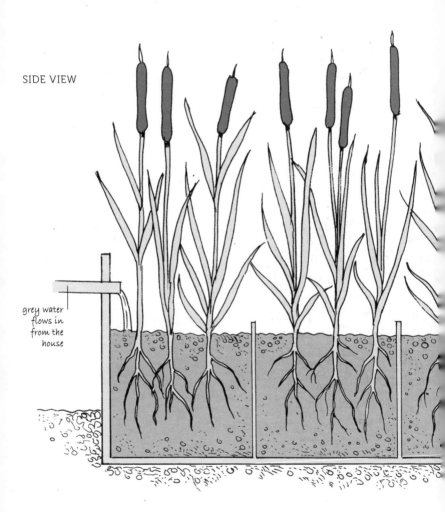

grey water flows in from the house

TOP VIEW

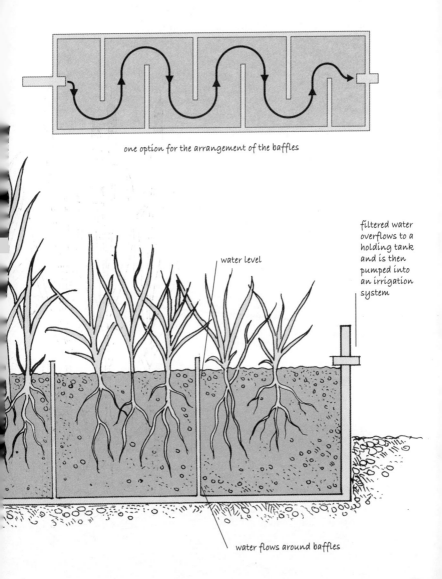

one option for the arrangement of the baffles

water level

filtered water overflows to a holding tank and is then pumped into an irrigation system

water flows around baffles

WASHING

Reducing your energy bills Whether you are doing the laundry or washing dishes, there are several simple strategies for minimising your consumption of hot water as well as saving energy.

THE LAUNDRY

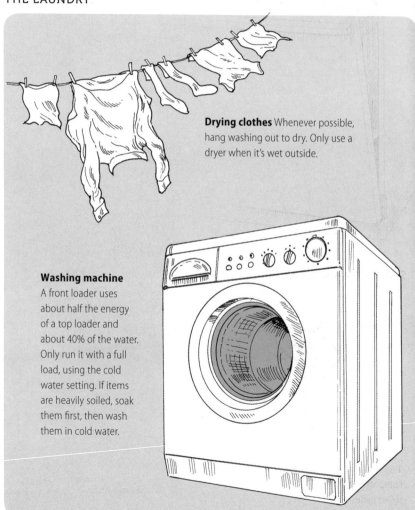

Drying clothes Whenever possible, hang washing out to dry. Only use a dryer when it's wet outside.

Washing machine A front loader uses about half the energy of a top loader and about 40% of the water. Only run it with a full load, using the cold water setting. If items are heavily soiled, soak them first, then wash them in cold water.

THE KITCHEN

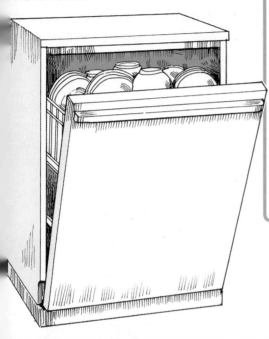

GENERAL TIPS

* Run the dishwasher when it's full, or choose the half-load option.
* Run it on the economy setting, which is shorter and uses less hot water.
* If your dishwasher has a heat-drying option, turn it off and open the door so the dishes dry naturally.
* Clean the filter regularly.

STACKING A DISHWASHER

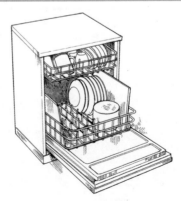

1 Scrape food scraps into the compost bin and rinse heavily soiled plates.

2 Working from back to front, and from the side to the middle, place smaller items on the top shelf. Put plates, pots and other heavily soiled items in the bottom shelf.

Lighting

Smart choices Maximising the amount of natural light in your home with windows and skylights will reduce your reliance on artificial light. You can also cut costs by choosing energy-efficient lighting.

TYPES OF LIGHTING

Fluorescent light tube
The conventional fluorescent tube requires special rectangular fittings but lasts up to 15 times longer than the incandescent light bulb.

Incandescent light bulb Conventional light bulbs are cheap but use a lot of energy to generate heat rather than light. You'll also need to replace them more often.

Halogen lamps These last twice as long as incandescent bulbs but you'll need transformers in the ceiling to operate them.

Compact fluorescent lamps (CFLs)
Unlike the fluoro tube, these can be fitted into an existing socket. They use about a quarter of the wattage of incandescent light bulbs.

SKYLIGHTS

Light and ventilation
Fitted with blinds, these can double as windows.

Skytubes A small tubular skylight, this reflects natural light through a diffuser – a practical choice for a dark hall.

DECORATIVE SKYLIGHT

STANDARD SKYLIGHT

SKYLIGHT WINDOW

Cooling and Heating

Utilising nature The cost of heating and cooling your home constitutes a significant chunk of your annual energy bill, so it is worthwhile considering some natural, and inexpensive, strategies.

Orientation Position a new house so that the living area faces the sun – in the northern hemisphere, it should face south, but the reverse in the southern hemisphere.

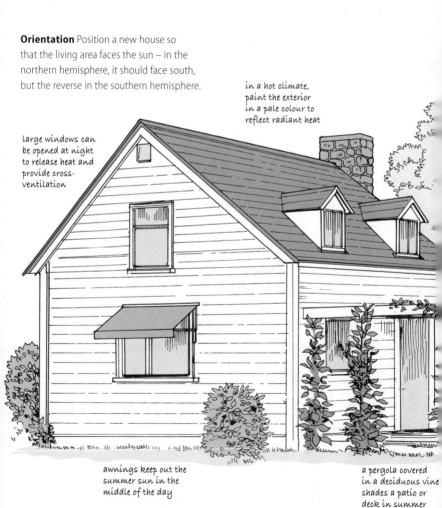

in a hot climate, paint the exterior in a pale colour to reflect radiant heat

large windows can be opened at night to release heat and provide cross-ventilation

awnings keep out the summer sun in the middle of the day

a pergola covered in a deciduous vine shades a patio or deck in summer

Light-filled villas
The ancient Romans oriented their houses so they faced the sun in winter, and even installed window panes of mica or glass.

deciduous trees provide shade in summer and admit the sun in winter

shrubs and trees don't absorb heat the way concrete does

Heating your house

The appropriate system Keeping your home warm in winter is a major cost. If you are building a new house, you could consider installing under-floor heating, a ground source heat pump or even heated windows.

STRATEGIES FOR KEEPING WARM

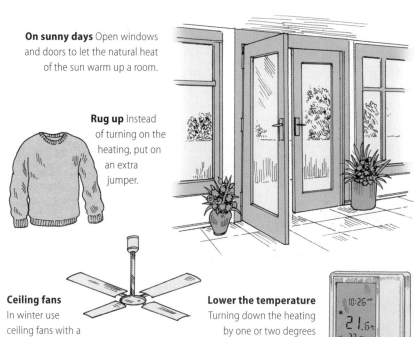

On sunny days Open windows and doors to let the natural heat of the sun warm up a room.

Rug up Instead of turning on the heating, put on an extra jumper.

Ceiling fans In winter use ceiling fans with a reverse function to direct rising heat downwards.

Lower the temperature Turning down the heating by one or two degrees can significantly reduce your energy bill.

CENTRAL HEATING

Piped heat There are several different types of central heating systems, including ducted, electric thin film and hydronic. Install a zoned system so you can close off rooms when they are not occupied.

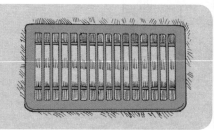

SPACE HEATING

Reverse cycle air conditioner If you live in a warm climate where the temperature does not drop below 5°C in winter, this may be the best option.

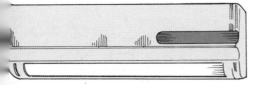

Wood fire The traditional open fire is inefficient and causes pollution. Most of the heat goes up the chimney.

Slow combustion wood fire Economical, especially if it is fitted with a fan, it is 60% more efficient than an open fire.

Bar heater Portable and cheap to buy, a bar heater is not only inefficient but also expensive to run.

Fan heater As with the bar heater, it is inefficient and expensive, but heats small rooms quickly.

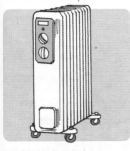

Oil-filled electric heater Castors make this type easy to move from room to room but it takes a while to warm up.

Flued gas heater Expensive to buy and install, it is cleaner and economical to run. Choose one without a pilot light.

Unflued gas heater Efficient and economical to run, this type requires ventilation to release the fumes.

Cooling options

Combating the heat For thousands of years humans have devised ingenious cooling systems. These days the excessive use of air conditioners, a culprit in the emission of greenhouse gases, can result in power blackouts.

A SHORT HISTORY OF AIR CONDITIONING

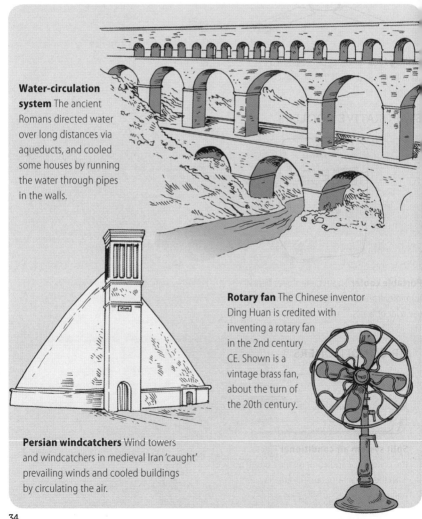

Water-circulation system The ancient Romans directed water over long distances via aqueducts, and cooled some houses by running the water through pipes in the walls.

Rotary fan The Chinese inventor Ding Huan is credited with inventing a rotary fan in the 2nd century CE. Shown is a vintage brass fan, about the turn of the 20th century.

Persian windcatchers Wind towers and windcatchers in medieval Iran 'caught' prevailing winds and cooled buildings by circulating the air.

ELECTRIC FANS

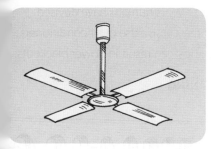

Ceiling fans Consider turning down the air conditioner and using the fan, which is much cheaper to run.

Portable fans Portable and cheap, they cool you down by directing moving air over the perspiration on your skin.

EVAPORATIVE COOLERS

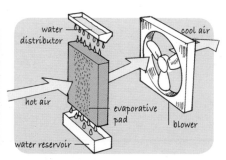

Portable cooler This type removes heat and humidity from a room but it is noisy and can use a lot of water.

How it works Hot air is drawn through a water-moistened filter and blown into the room as cool air.

AIR CONDITIONERS

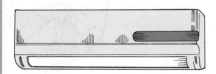

Split system air conditioner Pipes connect the condensor and compressor, housed outside, with the evaporator fan, the small wall-mounted unit inside.

Ducted air conditioning Install a zoned system so you can close off rooms when they are unoccupied.

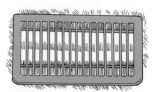

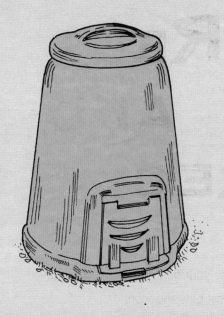

REUSE AND RECYCLE

Fertilise your garden with kitchen waste recycled in compost bins and worm farms, and discover how to 'make do' by finding new uses for everyday items, from the daily newspaper to a pair of tights.

Composting

Food for the garden Layer kitchen waste with garden prunings, grass clippings, newspaper and aged horse and cow manure until it rots down into nutrient-rich compost that can be used as fertiliser and mulch.

SOME GUIDELINES

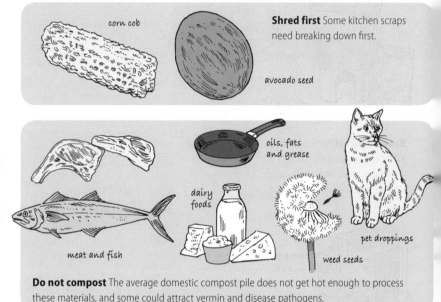

corn cob

avocado seed

Shred first Some kitchen scraps need breaking down first.

oils, fats and grease

dairy foods

meat and fish

weed seeds

pet droppings

Do not compost The average domestic compost pile does not get hot enough to process these materials, and some could attract vermin and disease pathogens.

MAKING COMPOST TEA

1 Place a spadeful of compost in a porous bag.

2 Steep it in a bucket of water for about 2 weeks.

3 Use the liquid fertiliser to water the roots of plants.

TYPES OF COMPOST BIN

Plastic bin Ideal for courtyard gardens, it should have a hatch for easy removal of the finished compost.

Compost tumbler Although this is the quickest way to produce compost, it takes some strength to rotate a fully laden bin.

Bokashi bucket Perfect for those living in an apartment, this unit uses a mix of sawdust and bran to process kitchen scraps.

Wire bin Use chicken wire and a few sturdy stakes to make a simple compost pile.

Three-bay compost A more elaborate enclosed system, which excludes vermin, allows you to manage compost in three stages.

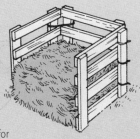

Compost bay Three recycled wooden pallets make a simple bay for garden waste. Tie the corners together with rope or wire.

WORM FARMS

A compact composting unit If you live in an apartment with a balcony, you can probably manage a worm farm, which typically comprises two or three plastic boxes containing tiger or red wiggler worms.

SETTING UP A WORM FARM

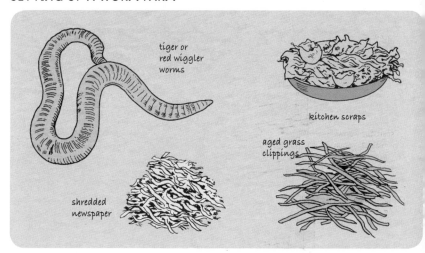

tiger or red wiggler worms

kitchen scraps

aged grass clippings

shredded newspaper

Tray 2 Bury kitchen scraps in some moist shredded newspaper and aged grass clippings. Monitor this layer a few times a week, adding food and occasionally water.

Tray 3 When the worms have eaten the contents of tray 2, entice the worms to tray 3 with more food scraps and bedding. When tray 2 is empty of worms, put the castings on the garden.

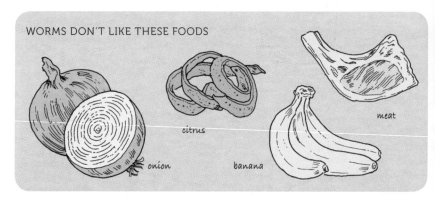

WORMS DON'T LIKE THESE FOODS

citrus

meat

onion

banana

HOW A WORM FARM WORKS

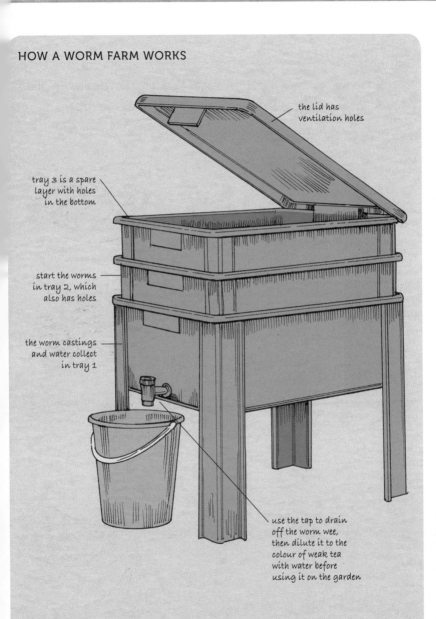

the lid has ventilation holes

tray 3 is a spare layer with holes in the bottom

start the worms in tray 2, which also has holes

the worm castings and water collect in tray 1

use the tap to drain off the worm wee, then dilute it to the colour of weak tea with water before using it on the garden

Sorting Recyclables

Reduce and recycle You may be surprised to learn how many common items can be safely recycled. If you are in doubt about a certain material, check with your local government authority before disposing of it.

RECYCLABLE HOUSEHOLD PRODUCTS

steel aerosol cans

glass bottles and jars

steel and aluminium cans

newspaper and other paper products

egg cartons

toilet rolls and other cardboard products

dairy and fruit juice cartons

plastic (PET) containers

metal bottle tops and lids

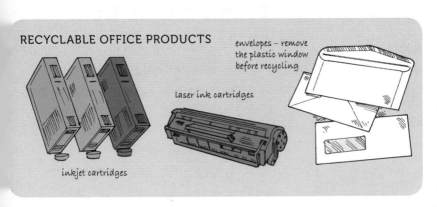

RECYCLABLE OFFICE PRODUCTS

envelopes – remove
the plastic window
before recycling

laser ink cartridges

inkjet cartridges

WHAT YOU CAN'T RECYCLE

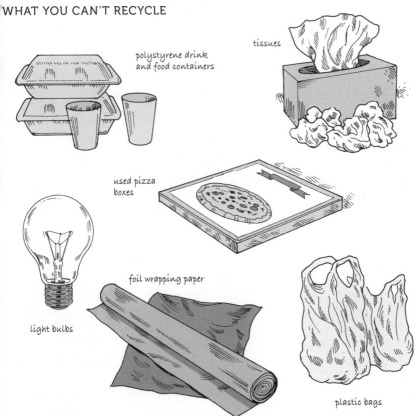

polystyrene drink
and food containers

tissues

used pizza
boxes

foil wrapping paper

light bulbs

plastic bags

Reusing containers

A new purpose Even if your local government authority offers a recycling service, you can help save the energy required for the manufacture and transport of new containers by finding new purposes for common items.

STORAGE IDEAS

Craft supplies Old jam jars can hold buttons and ribbon.

Travelling sewing kit An old tobacco tin is the ideal size.

Empty packaging Give children empty cereal boxes so they can play 'shop'.

Paper lantern Cut a design in a takeaway carton and place a candle inside.

String dispenser Store a ball of string in an old teapot.

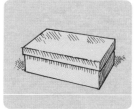

Shoebox Use it to file photos, craft supplies and bills.

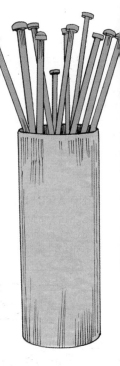

Knitting needles Store them in cylindrical containers.

NEW USES

Vases and candle-holders
Convert decorative glass jars and bottles.

Garden scoop Cut the bottom and one side from a 2-litre bottle.

Plastic funnel
Cut the top off a plastic drink bottle and use the pouring end as a funnel.

Water bottles Cut the bottoms off, attach an aqua spike to each spout and insert them next to plants.

Biodegradable pots Plant seeds in egg cartons. Once seedlings appear, plant the whole thing.

Mini cloche Cut off the bottom of a plastic soft-drink bottle, remove the lid and use it to cover a seedling.

MAKING A TIN LIGHT

1 To prevent the tin from collapsing, fill a clean, empty tin with water and freeze it. Attach a paper pattern.

2 Use a hammer and nail to make the pattern.

3 Remove the pattern and place a candle inside.

10 USES FOR NEWSPAPER

A useful resource Here are just some of the practical and creative ways you can reuse newspaper, and at the same time reduce your reliance on plastic products and chemical cleaners in your home.

AROUND THE HOUSE

Firestarters Tightly roll up a sheet of a broadsheet newspaper, fold it in half and twist it tightly. Tie off with a piece of string.

Clean a barbecue Remove the messy residue with scrunched up newspaper.

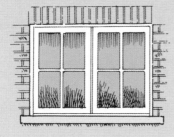

Polish windows After cleaning windows, use scrunched up newspaper to polish the glass.

Kitchen cupboards Spread several sheets of newspaper on top of kitchen cupboards – they will catch grease and save you the effort of cleaning.

Pets Spread sheets of newspaper on the floor of a dog kennel or use them to line a kitty litter tray.

CRAFT IDEAS

Coiled bowl Dip strips of newspaper in glue, hang to dry, then wet them and coil them into a bowl shape.

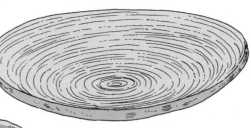

Papier-mâché Paste overlapped strips of newspaper onto a mould, such as a bowl, and decorate it when it is dry.

IN THE GARDEN

Newspaper strips Tear sheets of newspaper into strips and add them to the compost pile.

Garden mulch Spread at least 15 layers of newspaper between two layers of manure, add a layer of organic mulch and water well.

Seedling pots Plant seedlings, pot and all.

Hazardous waste

Don't contaminate the environment Check with your local government authority to find out how to safely dispose of heavy metals, electronic parts and dangerous chemicals, such as refrigerants.

CHEMICALS

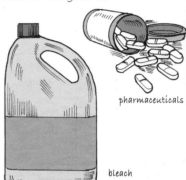

pharmaceuticals

engine oil

paint

bleach

ELECTRONIC GOODS

computer

mobile phone

batteries – those containing heavy metals may be recyclable

CERAMICS AND CERTAIN TYPES OF GLASS

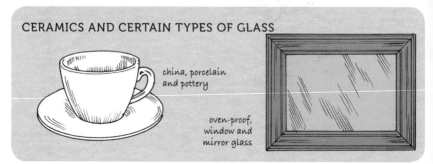

china, porcelain and pottery

oven-proof, window and mirror glass

WHITE GOODS AND OTHER APPLIANCES

Sewing Basics

The essentials Armed with a small sewing kit and a few basic stitches, you can extend the life of your clothes by repairing hems, sewing on buttons and replacing zippers, or even embellishing with simple embroidery.

BASIC SEWING KIT

Pins To prevent rusting, store them in a small container with 1 teaspoon of talcum powder.

Needles Keep a variety, including sewing, darning and embroidery needles.

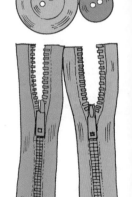

Scissors Keep them sharp with a knife sharpener.

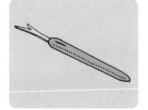

Thimble This is an essential tool for protecting your finger while you sew.

Fasteners Include zips, press studs and hooks and eyes.

Tape measure Choose one that has both metric and imperial measurements.

Unpicker An indispensible tool for unpicking stitches and cutting seams.

Thread Include black, white, navy, red and beige so you can make running repairs.

USEFUL STITCHES

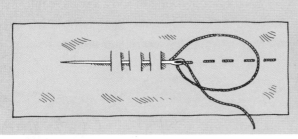

running stitch, for gathering – weave the needle in and out of the fabric to make stitches that are smaller than tacking stitch (see below)

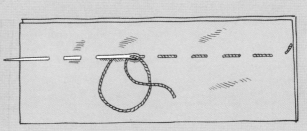

tacking or basting stitch, for temporarily sewing together two pieces of fabric while you fit a garment – make each stitch about 6 mm long

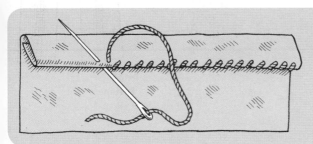

hemming stitch, for finishing raw edges – fold the raw edge under and secure to the fabric with a slanting stitch

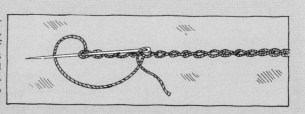

chain stitch, for embroidery – you can also use this series of looped stitches on its own to make a thread chain for a small button loop

Simple sewing repairs

Running repairs Do you throw out garments once they develop a small hole or tear, or lose a button? Some sewing repairs may take a little practice but they will make your clothes last longer and save you money.

DARNING

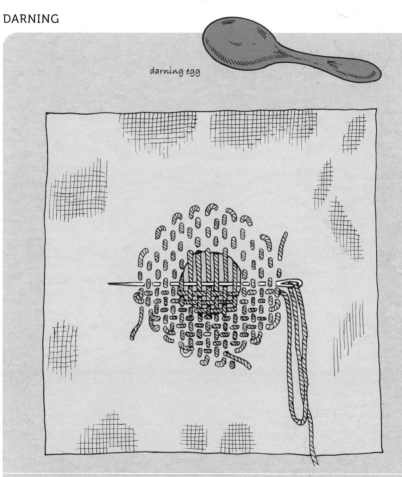

darning egg

How to darn a small hole With the hole over the darning egg, and using a small tacking stitch, sew in both directions, allowing a generous margin around the hole. As you sew at right angles to the vertical rows of stitching, weave the needle over and under.

SEWING ON A BUTTON

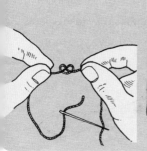

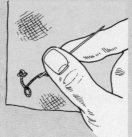

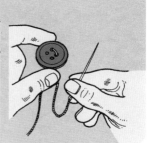

1 Thread the needle, then tie a knot.

2 Anchor the stitch, then repeat steps 3–5 several times.

3 Pull the thread through the button.

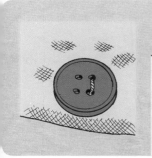

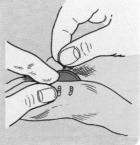

4 Sew the first 2 holes.

5 Repeat on the other holes.

6 To finish, push the needle through to the wrong side.

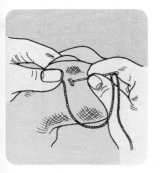

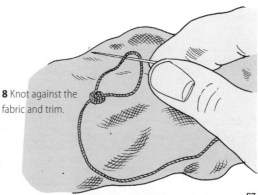

8 Knot against the fabric and trim.

7 Push the needle through all the stitches.

Making do

'Waste not, want not' Economic depressions and wartime shortages forced previous generations to develop lots of clever but simple ways to 'make do'. Reduce your contribution to landfill with these ideas.

THRIFTINESS IN WARTIME

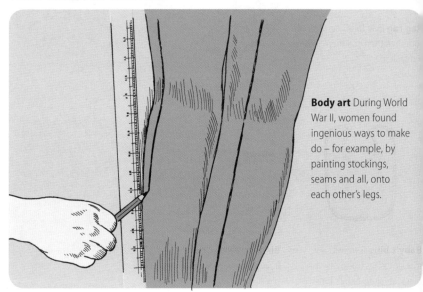

Body art During World War II, women found ingenious ways to make do – for example, by painting stockings, seams and all, onto each other's legs.

SOFT FURNISHINGS

Cushion covers When curtains are past their best, turn the most vibrant part of the fabric into cushion covers.

Felt patchwork Wash old woollen garments until they felt, then cut them into squares and sew them together to make patchwork rugs and cushion covers.

MISCELLANEOUS ITEMS

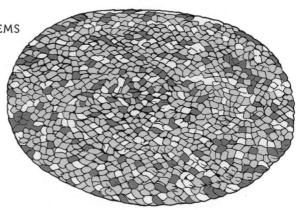

Rag rug Plait fabric scraps together, then coil them into a rug shape.

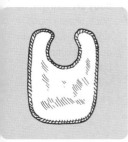

Baby's bibs Turn old mackintoshes (rubberised raincoats) into baby's bibs.

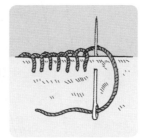

Blanket stitch Tidy up the frayed edge of a blanket with blanket stitch.

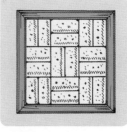

Trivet Glue wine corks of the same size onto a piece of board and frame it.

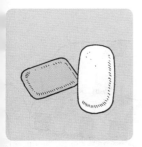

Soap scraps Cover with water, add a little borax and boil for a few minutes, stirring. When cool, cut into blocks.

Gift tags Recycle old birthday cards into place names and gift tags, and old Christmas cards into tree decorations.

Face washer Cut a frayed towel into pieces, each the size of a face washer, and trim with braid.

CLOTHING

Recycled jeans When the knees go on a favourite pair of jeans, cut off the legs and wear them as shorts, or sew them into a skirt.

Sock puppet Turn an odd sock into a hand puppet with button eyes and wool hair.

New trim Brighten or update a cardigan with new buttons or trim.

Natural dyes Revive faded fabrics with seed, fruit and vegetable dyes, such as coffee and beetroot.

REUSING KNITTING WOOL

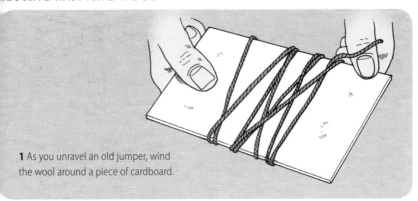

1 As you unravel an old jumper, wind the wool around a piece of cardboard.

2 Insert 2 wooden spoons between the wool and cardboard, then remove the cardboard and hold the wool over a bowl of steaming water until it is damp.

3 When the wool is dry, wind it into a ball.

10 USES FOR TIGHTS

Longer lives When ladders and snags develop in your tights, pantyhose or stockings, don't throw them out – there are lots of practical ways to use them in the house and garden.

AROUND THE HOUSE

Soap scrubber Place a bar of soap in the cut-off toe of a stocking leg, secure it with string and hang it from the laundry or garden tap.

Tennis pole Hammer a strong stake into the ground. Put a tennis ball into the toe of a stocking leg and secure the other end to the top of the pole.

Furniture polisher Use a balled pair of tights to polish furniture.

Paint strainer Remove dust and debris from paint by pouring it through a stocking strainer.

Lost contact lens
Stretch a piece of stocking nylon over the nozzle of a vacuum cleaner, secure it with string and vacuum the floor. The nylon will prevent the lens from being sucked into the dust bag.

IN THE GARDEN

Sprouts strainer To strain sprouts after washing them, stretch a piece of stocking over the neck of the container and secure with a rubber band.

Water wick Wind a strip of old stocking around the root ball of a pot plant, leaving a 'tail'. Replace the plant in its pot, and put the tail in a bowl of water.

Plant tie Use stocking legs to stake a tree or support a tall flower or vegetable, such as a tomato plant or dahlia.

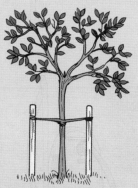

Bulb storage Use the legs of a pair of tights to store onions, garlic and flower bulbs. Knot the nylon between each bulb so it won't rot.

Melon support To prevent a developing melon or pumpkin from rotting on the ground, place it in a stocking leg, tie off the top and suspend it from a strong support.

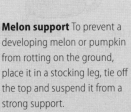

CLEANING THE HOUSE

With a green cleaning kit, you can clean every room in the house without resorting to chemical cleaners. Not only will you have a safer, cleaner home but the environment will also benefit.

CHEMICALS IN THE HOME

If you must use chemicals If you're stripping lead paint, spraying fruit trees or using chemical cleaners, which we don't recommend, always wear protective clothing, and work outside or in an area with plenty of ventilation.

PERSONAL PROTECTION

plenty of ventilation

goggles

mask

rubber gloves

long sleeves

SOURCES OF VOLATILE ORGANIC COMPOUNDS (VOCs)

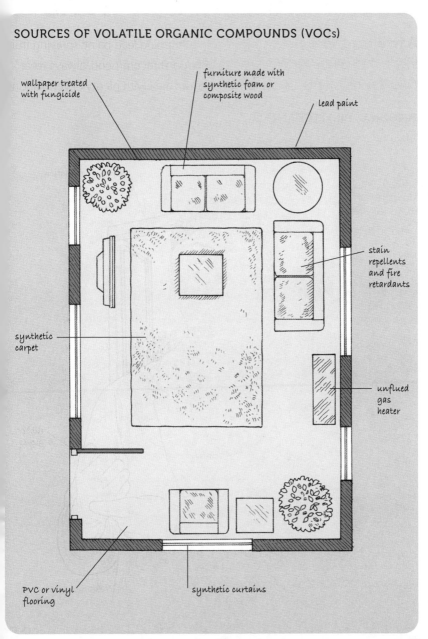

wallpaper treated with fungicide

furniture made with synthetic foam or composite wood

lead paint

stain repellents and fire retardants

synthetic carpet

unflued gas heater

PVC or vinyl flooring

synthetic curtains

CLEAN AIR

A healthy home Have you ever wondered why so many offices rent indoor plants? They not only bring the garden inside but also clean the air by absorbing harmful chemicals in the atmosphere.

NATURAL AIR FRESHENERS

Strewing herbs In the Middle Ages fragrant herbs such as lavender were cast on the floor to mask the smell of unwashed bodies.

Heat essential oils Use a burner or vaporiser.

Mask cooking smells Boil 8 cloves in 2 cups water.

Make a pomander Stick cloves into an orange and cure in newspaper for 1 week.

Potpourri Tuck sachets between sofa cushions.

NDOOR PLANTS

cus benjamina Weeping fig,
hardy indoor plant with glossy
aves, tolerates neglect.

Dracaena marginata Keep
the strappy leaves clean by
wiping them regularly with
a damp cloth.

Philodendron 'Xanadu' This
attractive plant, with its lush
foliage, needs lots of light
when it's grown indoors.

Spathiphyllum wallisii The
peace lily produces sculptural
white flowers and broad,
glossy green leaves.

Green cleaning kit

Simple, safe and effective Throw out all those expensive proprietary cleaning products and put together your own green cleaning kit with some household tools and common ingredients from your pantry.

ESSENTIAL TOOLS

dust pan and brush

duster

rubber gloves

toothbrush and scrubbing brush

vacuum cleaner

mop, bucket and a stiff or soft broom

lint-free cleaning cloths

CLEANING SOLUTIONS

vinegar and lemon

washing soda

bicarbonate of soda

borax

eucalyptus oil

salt

USEFUL EXTRAS

pure soap flakes are 100% biodegradable

glycerine helps dissolve various forms of dirt

shoe polish masks scratches on timber

BICARBONATE OF SODA

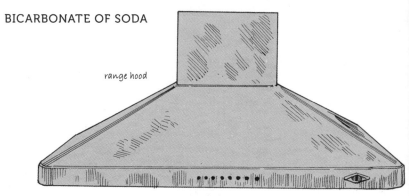

range hood

Super cleaner Use bicarb for many cleaning jobs. Mix it with water to make a paste.

chrome and stainless steel

plastic toys

tea and coffee stains

Absorb odours Put a small bowl of bicarbonate of soda in the fridge.

Silver Soak silver cutlery on a layer of aluminium foil in a warm solution of bicarb.

Oven Clean a warm oven with bicarb paste and and leave it on overnight. Wipe off.

WASHING SODA

clear a blocked drain

clean the oven

descale a kettle

clean tarnished silver

clean dirty oven racks

soften washing water

revitalise kitchen sponges

SALT

Natural scourer Use table salt with a little water or lemon juice to scour kitchen items.

Condition a new bristle broom Soak it in hot salty water for 20 minutes, then dry. It will last longer.

BORAX

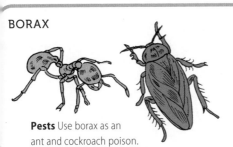

Pests Use borax as an ant and cockroach poison.

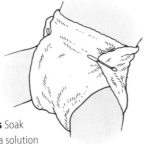

Nappies Soak them in a solution of ½ cup borax to a bucket of water.

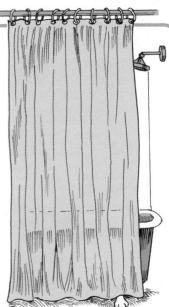

Mould Scrub a mouldy shower curtain with a paste of borax and lemon juice.

Clean toilet Pour 1 cup borax and ¼ cup white vinegar in the bowl.

Whiter whites Add ½ cup borax to a very hot wash.

LEMON

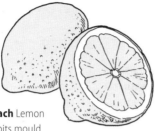

Mild bleach Lemon juice inhibits mould as well as deodorises and removes stains.

Cutlery stains Dissolve a little salt in lemon juice and rub.

Polish a copper pan Rub the pan with half a lemon dipped in salt.

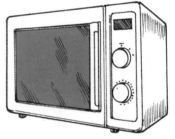

Clean a microwave oven Cook the juice of 1 lemon in a bowl on High for 5 minutes.

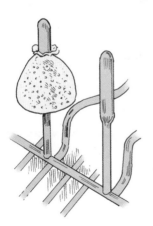

Greasy dishwasher load Cut a lemon in half, remove the seeds and skewer the cut side of each half onto the spikes of the plate rack.

Deodorise the bin Wash with a solution of 1 teaspoon lemon juice to 2 litres water.

WHITE VINEGAR

Brighten a dishwasher
Run empty on a short cycle with 1 cup vinegar in the machine.

Unblock a drain Put 1 cup vinegar and ¼ cup bicarbonate of soda down the drain and replace the plug for 10 minutes. Run the tap to rinse.

Smelly plastic contaner Wipe over with cloth dipped in white vinegar.

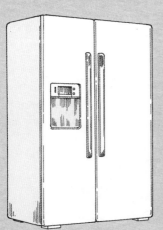

Clean a dirty vase
Fill it with white vinegar. For stubborn stains add rice, cover and shake.

Remove labels and decals
Soak the item with vinegar for 10 minutes then peel off. Repeat if necessary.

Prevent mould Wipe over interior of fridge with vinegar.

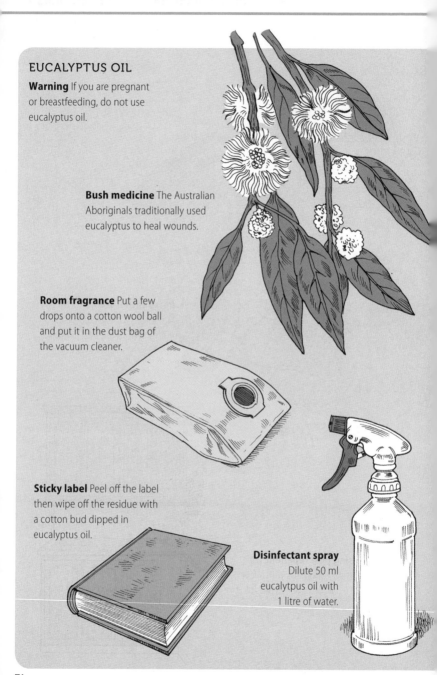

EUCALYPTUS OIL

Warning If you are pregnant or breastfeeding, do not use eucalyptus oil.

Bush medicine The Australian Aboriginals traditionally used eucalyptus to heal wounds.

Room fragrance Put a few drops onto a cotton wool ball and put it in the dust bag of the vacuum cleaner.

Sticky label Peel off the label then wipe off the residue with a cotton bud dipped in eucalyptus oil.

Disinfectant spray Dilute 50 ml eucalyptus oil with 1 litre of water.

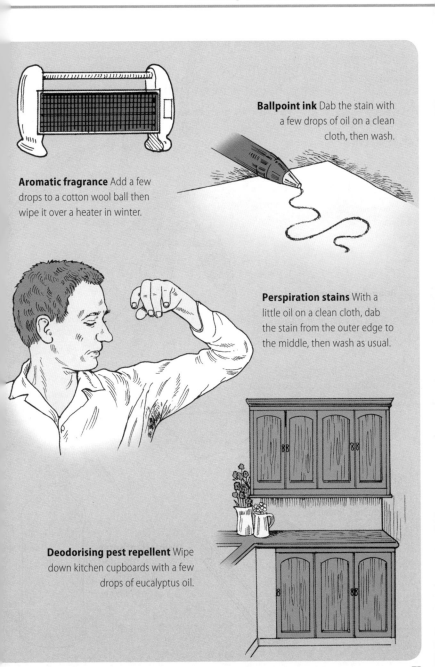

Aromatic fragrance Add a few drops to a cotton wool ball then wipe it over a heater in winter.

Ballpoint ink Dab the stain with a few drops of oil on a clean cloth, then wash.

Perspiration stains With a little oil on a clean cloth, dab the stain from the outer edge to the middle, then wash as usual.

Deodorising pest repellent Wipe down kitchen cupboards with a few drops of eucalyptus oil.

CLEANING ROUTINE

Household management It's easy to keep on top of housework tasks by devising a simple routine and sticking to it. If you have young children and pets, you may need to clean the house more often than once a week.

DAILY TASKS

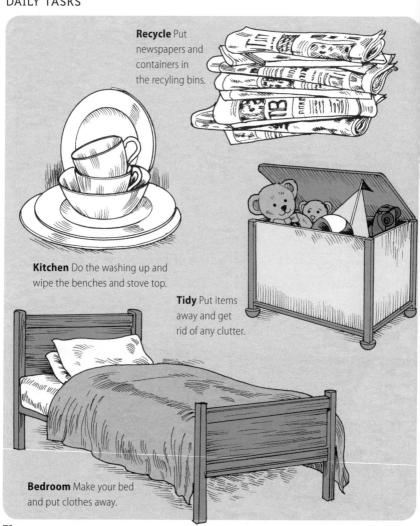

Recycle Put newspapers and containers in the recyling bins.

Kitchen Do the washing up and wipe the benches and stove top.

Tidy Put items away and get rid of any clutter.

Bedroom Make your bed and put clothes away.

WEEKLY TASKS

Washing Change the sheets and towels, and do the washing.

Clean the house Dust, mop and vacuum.

Kitchen bin Empty and clean it.

SEASONAL TASKS

Wardrobe Organise clothes.

Windows Wash them inside and out.

Fridge Clean it out.

Dust mites

Out of sight A mattress that's been in use for a couple of years may harbour up to two million dust mites, which cause serious health problems such as asthma and allergies, so protect your home with these strategies.

HOW TO DISCOURAGE DUST MITES

Freeze them out Kill dust mites by putting soft toys in the freezer for 24 hours.

Steam clean Regularly clean soft furnishings and carpets by having them steam cleaned.

Air the bedding As often as you can, hang out the bedding to air on warm, sunny days.

Reduce clutter Keep books and ornaments dust-free behind closed doors.

THE BEDROOM

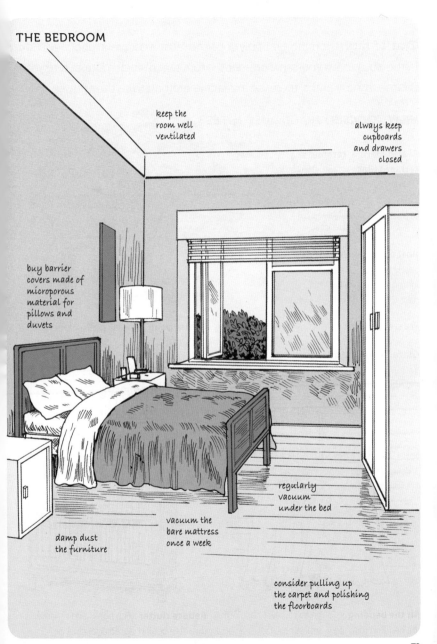

keep the room well ventilated

always keep cupboards and drawers closed

buy barrier covers made of microporous material for pillows and duvets

regularly vacuum under the bed

vacuum the bare mattress once a week

damp dust the furniture

consider pulling up the carpet and polishing the floorboards

Hard floors

Traffic flow Flooring probably cops the most wear and tear of any surface in the house so, if you can, consider the function of each room before you choose the coverings, then use a cleaning method to suit the finish.

TILED FLOORS

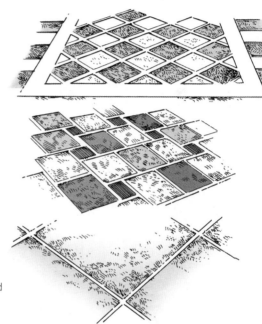

Sealed marble, ceramic or terrazzo tiles Vacuum, then mop with a solution of 2 cups vinegar per bucket of warm water. Do not use acids on unsealed marble.

Rust stains on ceramic tiles Saturate an absorbent cloth with lemon juice and a few drops of detergent. Lay it on the stain for a few hours, then rinse.

Glazed slate and quarry tiles Vacuum and mop with a mild detergent solution. Polish unglazed tiles with wax polish.

CUTTING A CERAMIC TILE FOR REPAIRS

1 Using a straight edge on a flat surface, score the tile with a tile cutter.

2 With the scored line over a small piece of dowel, press on both sides.

3 To cut a narrow piece, score the tile, then break off bits with a pair of pincers.

TIMBER FLOORS

Finishes Timber flooring needs protection in the form of varnish (either natural or synthetic), wax, oil or wood stain. Vacuum dirt and grit before damp mopping.

Leave shoes at the door
Wear house slippers or just socks or stockings inside your home.

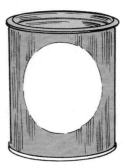

Oil-finished timber
After sweeping or vacuuming, mop with a solution of 1 part methylated spirits to 10 parts warm water.

VINYL AND LINOLEUM

Vinyl Clean vinyl flooring with a mix of ¼ cup pure soap flakes, ½ cup bicarb and 2 cups warm water.

Linoleum Vacuum and damp mop. To polish, rub with raw linseed oil, leave for half an hour, then dry with a clean cloth.

CARING FOR TIMBER FLOORS

Protection Just one party can wreak havoc on a timber floor, but most mishaps can be easily fixed. One exception is possibly the stiletto heel – if you don't want to ask your guests to remove them, provide them with caps.

QUICK FIXES

Oil and grease
Use fine steel wool moistened with mineral turpentine to buff the timber with the grain.

Shallow cigarette burn If the floor does not have a hard finish, moisten steel wool with wax and rub. For a hard finish, buy a touch-up kit and refinish.

Dents Repair a few small marks by using steel wool to rub in wax, then buff. Or try steaming the mark with an iron but the water may damage the floor further.

Water mark Pass a dry iron over a clean cotton cloth for several seconds. Keep checking and ironing until the stain is gone.

Scratches and cuts Apply cleaning solvent on steel wool, then rinse and refinish.

PROTECTING THE FLOOR AND REDUCING NOISE

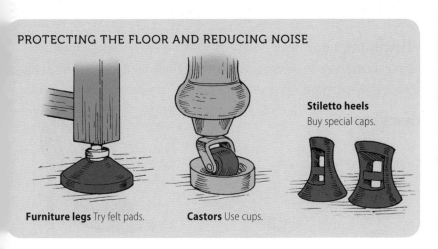

Furniture legs Try felt pads.

Castors Use cups.

Stiletto heels
Buy special caps.

FIXING A SQUEAKY FLOORBOARD

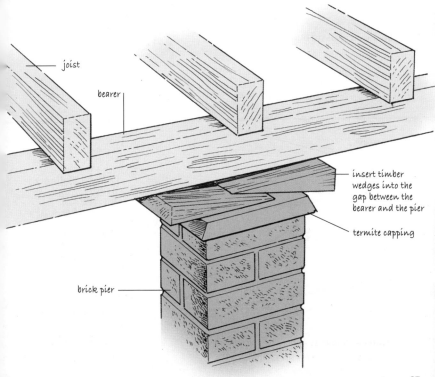

joist

bearer

insert timber
wedges into the
gap between the
bearer and the pier

termite capping

brick pier

CARPET AND RUGS

Warmth and comfort With proper care, carpet and rugs should last for years, especially if they are of good quality. Act quickly to treat spills and other accidents, but when you're in doubt, call in the professionals.

CARPET CARE

Carpet beater Before vacuum cleaners became affordable in the mid-19th century, rugs and carpets were hung over a railing or the washing line and beaten with a carpet beater.

Castor cups To avoid having permanent dents in your carpet, place castor cups under furniture legs.

Valuable rugs Vacuum them with reduced suction, in the direction of the pile.

Restore the pile To raise the pile in a dent, place an ice cube on it.

Steam cleaning This not only deep-cleans the carpet but also removes carpet beetle and dust mite droppings and flakes of human skin.

STAIN REMOVAL

Red wine Blot with paper towels, then sprinkle with white wine. Blot again. Remove what's left with methylated spirits on a clean cloth.

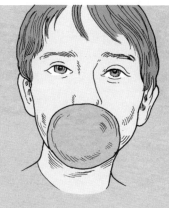

Chewing gum Apply a small bag of ice for 15 minutes, then peel off. Sponge residue with dry-cleaning solvent, then diluted detergent.

Coffee stains Rub with a solution of borax and warm water.

Candle wax Use a blunt knife to scrape off as much as you can, then hot iron over blotting paper.

Pet urine Blot with paper towel, then sprinkle over bicarbonate of soda. Allow to dry, then vacuum.

Walls

Blank canvas If you can't remove a mark or stain from a painted wall, you can always paint over it, but if your walls are covered with wallpaper, you'll need to monitor their condition more closely.

WALLPAPER

Spot clean
Dust wallpaper with powdered borax, then brush it off.

Marks on wallpaper Rub off with a piece of bread.

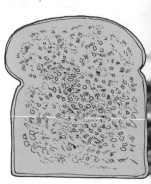

Remove old wallpaper Roll on a solution of 1 part white vinegar to 1 part warm water, then scrape off.

PAINTED WALLS

dust painted walls and remove cobwebs with a cloth tied over a soft broom

clean crayon and pen marks with a paste of bicarb and water

wash off mould with a solution of white vinegar and warm water

Sinks and basins

Safety measure Sooner or later you'll need to unblock a drain, or search for a lost item in the kitchen trap. Both jobs are easy to do, as long as you have the right tools and turn off the mains water before touching the pipes.

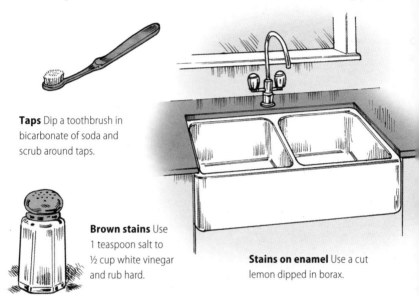

Taps Dip a toothbrush in bicarbonate of soda and scrub around taps.

Brown stains Use 1 teaspoon salt to ½ cup white vinegar and rub hard.

Stains on enamel Use a cut lemon dipped in borax.

RETRIEVING JEWELLERY

1 Turn off the water. Put a bucket under the trap.

2 Loosen the nuts on the trap.

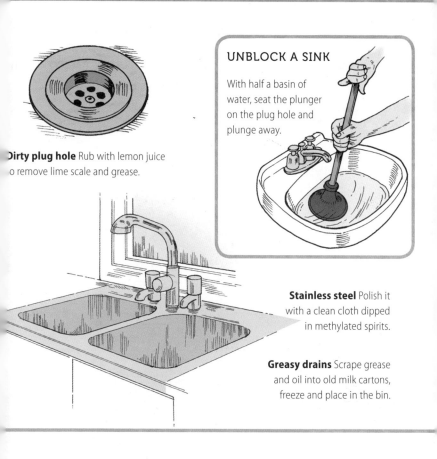

Dirty plug hole Rub with lemon juice to remove lime scale and grease.

UNBLOCK A SINK

With half a basin of water, seat the plunger on the plug hole and plunge away.

Stainless steel Polish it with a clean cloth dipped in methylated spirits.

Greasy drains Scrape grease and oil into old milk cartons, freeze and place in the bin.

3 Remove the trap and retrieve the item.

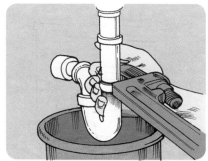

4 Reattach the trap.

SHOWERS AND BATHS

Elbow grease To prevent a build-up of grime that can be hard to remove without a lot of hard scrubbing, wipe down the bath and shower surfaces every few days.

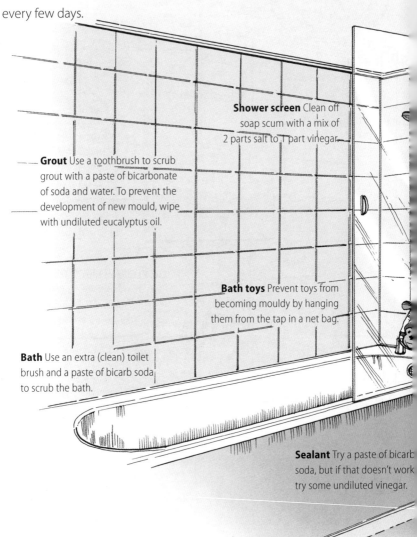

Shower screen Clean off soap scum with a mix of 2 parts salt to 1 part vinegar.

Grout Use a toothbrush to scrub grout with a paste of bicarbonate of soda and water. To prevent the development of new mould, wipe with undiluted eucalyptus oil.

Bath toys Prevent toys from becoming mouldy by hanging them from the tap in a net bag.

Bath Use an extra (clean) toilet brush and a paste of bicarb soda to scrub the bath.

Sealant Try a paste of bicarb soda, but if that doesn't work try some undiluted vinegar.

Extractor fan Prevent mould forming by removing steam with a fan.

Mirror Use a solution of strained tea leaves and water.

Lime scale on taps Soak a cloth in white vinegar and wrap it around the taps for about half an hour. Rinse.

Soap scum, body fats and oils in the pipes Use a product that is recommended by the manufacturer.

SHOWER

Built up lime Remove the head, soak in white vinegar overnight, then scrub with a toothbrush before replacing.

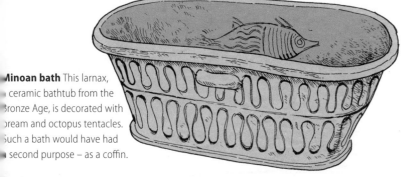

Minoan bath This larnax, a ceramic bathtub from the Bronze Age, is decorated with bream and octopus tentacles. Such a bath would have had a second purpose – as a coffin.

REGROUTING

1 Go over the old grout with a grout rake or screwdriver. Wipe off any loose grout.

2 Mix some grout powder to the consistency of toothpaste, then apply it.

3 After a few hours, use a damp cloth to wipe off the excess grout.

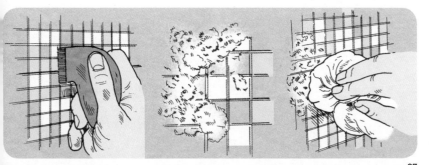

Homemade toiletries

Garden fresh There are many simple herbal preparations that can soothe or invigorate, delighting your senses with their fragrance. Before trying a new herb, patch test a small amount on the inside of your arm.

HERBAL BATHS

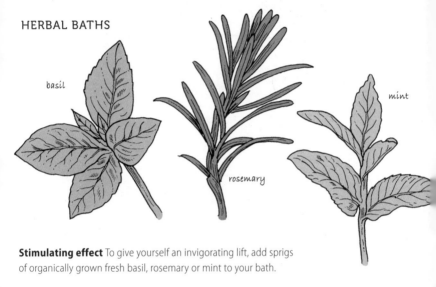

basil

rosemary

mint

Stimulating effect To give yourself an invigorating lift, add sprigs of organically grown fresh basil, rosemary or mint to your bath.

MAKING A SOOTHING BATH BAG

1 Fill a small muslin bag, available from craft shops, with rolled oats.

2 Add some rose petals and lavender flowers, or choose another combination.

3 Pull the string tight. Tie it under the tap or add it to the bath.

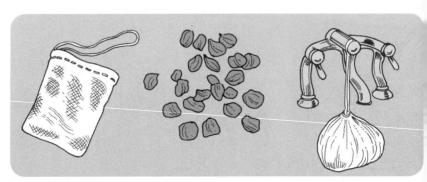

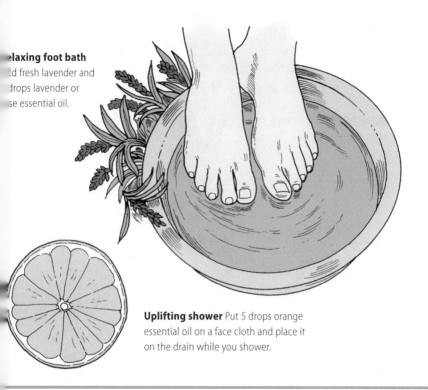

laxing foot bath
d fresh lavender and
drops lavender or
se essential oil.

Uplifting shower Put 5 drops orange essential oil on a face cloth and place it on the drain while you shower.

MAKING CITRUS BATH BOMBS

1 In a bowl, mix ½ cup citric acid with 1 cup bicarbonate of soda.

2 Add 10 drops orange essential oil and enough witch hazel to moisten.

3 Pack into flexible muffin moulds and leave overnight before turning out.

TOILET ISSUES

The smallest room Even the toilet can be a pleasant space if you keep it spotlessly clean and take the trouble to add simple but thoughtful touches such as a scented candle and something to read.

CLEANING THE TOILET

borax

vinegar

toilet brush

Natural stain remover Mix together 1 cup borax and ¼ cup white vinegar and pour into the toilet bowl. Leave overnight, then give the bowl a good scrub.

DEODORISING THE TOILET

Courtesy match Strike a match (or light a candle) over the bowl.

Scented candle When you have house guests, put one on the vanity and keep it alight.

UNCLOGGING A TOILET

Turn off the water supply to the toilet and remove as much water as you can.

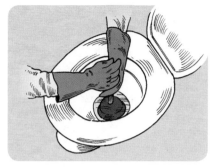

2 Use the plunger, doing your best to maintain the seal.

3 Unbend a coat hanger and try twisting it into the blockage.

4 Remove the wire, and insert a drain snake or plumber's eel.

5 Rotate and pull the eel by turns to loosen the blockage.

6 Once the water starts to drain, flush the toilet. Check it drains properly.

FURNITURE AND LIGHTING

You can create a sanctuary of comfort with a beautifully maintained home – keep timber furniture polished, upholstery and curtains clean and dust-free, and mirrors and windows sparkling clean.

UPHOLSTERED FURNITURE

Home comforts Grime, grease and stains on fabric and leather not only look unsightly but also shorten the life of upholstered furniture, particularly if it's covered in fabric, which is cheaper than leather but not as robust.

FABRIC UPHOLSTERY

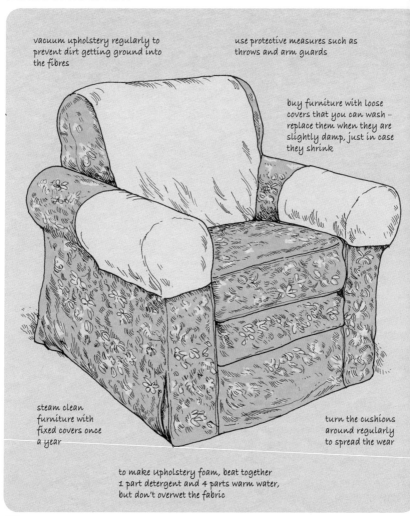

vacuum upholstery regularly to prevent dirt getting ground into the fibres

use protective measures such as throws and arm guards

buy furniture with loose covers that you can wash – replace them when they are slightly damp, just in case they shrink

steam clean furniture with fixed covers once a year

turn the cushions around regularly to spread the wear

to make upholstery foam, beat together 1 part detergent and 4 parts warm water, but don't overwet the fabric

LEATHER UPHOLSTERY

Leather furniture Better for the allergy-prone, as it doesn't harbour dust mites to the same extent as fabric, leather upholstery also tends to withstand pets and boisterous children better.

GENERAL TIPS

* Clean minor stains and spills with a damp cloth.
* Clean stains with a solution of 2 tablespoons white vinegar to 1 bucket water, then dry thoroughly.
* Polish with a cloth dipped in a solution of 1 part vinegar to 2 parts linseed oil.

TIMBER FURNITURE

Valuable investment Whether it's finished with wax, oil, lacquer or French polish, keep timber furniture looking good by protecting it from damage and also by using the right techniques to clean and maintain it.

GENERAL TIPS

* Protect a timber table with mats and trivets or heat pads.
* Position timber furniture away from direct heat, which can dry out the wood and cause cracking.
* When removing stains and repairing damage, use the gentlest solution first.

MAINTENANCE TIPS

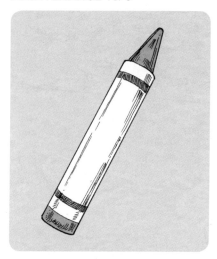

Scratch Mask with colour-matched shoe polish or wax crayon. Once it is absorbed, buff.

Fingerprints Wipe them with a damp cloth dipped in a detergent solution.

Marks left by drink containers Rub some cream metal polish in the direction of the grain, then polish with wax.

Waxed timber Dust it first or the wax will seal in dirt and abrade the surface. Use a solid wax (cream waxes contain solvents). When dry, buff.

SIMPLE REPAIRS

French polish To remove this finish when restoring, rub with fine steel wool dipped in methylated spirits.

Sticky drawer Rub candle wax along the drawer runners and sides. If that doesn't help, check the drawer is square and repair it if necessary.

'REPURPOSING' FURNITURE

Beyond recycling Next time you encounter an appealing piece of furniture that needs repair or restoration, think beyond the obvious – consider how it could be reinvented with a new purpose or function.

BOOKSHELVES

Bench seats Stack three on top of each other to make a more elegant version of the brick and plank bookcase.

WARDROBE CONVERSION

Old wardrobe
Convert the storage drawer into a coffee table and the original hanging space above into a bookcase with glass doors.

Sideboard Revamp a beautiful sideboard into a bathroom cabinet.

DECORATIVE BEDHEAD

Antique railing Transform a section of antique railing, or a pair of panelled doors, into a decorative bedhead.

BEDSIDE TABLE

Sewing machine table Remove some of the operating mechanism and fit it with a new top.

Window treatments

Light and heat control Curtains and blinds have several functions – they can decorate a room and provide you with privacy while excluding the heat of the summer sun or minimising heat loss on a cold winter's night.

CLEANING BLINDS AND CURTAINS

Roman blind Take it down, draw a 'map' of the strings and remove them. Wash as for the roller blind (opposite), then reassemble.

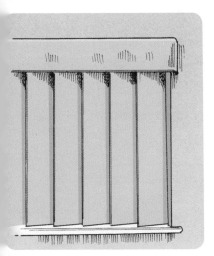

Vertical blinds Remove the blades, stacking as you go, and soak them in a solution of washing detergent and cold water. Hang to dry, using towels on the floor to catch the drips.

Venetian blinds Vacuum first, with the slats in both directions. Then, wearing a pair of old fabric gloves dipped in warm soapy water, run your fingers along each slat, top and bottom.

Velvet curtains Brush them with a stiff brush to remove any dust and lint, then hang them over a hot bath to restore the pile. Rather than fold them, rehang them immediately.

Roller blind To wash, unroll into a bath of warm water and detergent, sponging as you go. Rinse in the same way. Hang the dripping blind on the line, then dry it with towels.

WINDOW REPAIRS

Do it yourself Here are some simple repairs to double-hung windows and flyscreens that you can do yourself, regardless of your skill level. All you need are a few tools and a spare half-hour.

FIXING A BALKY SASH ON A DOUBLE-HUNG WINDOW

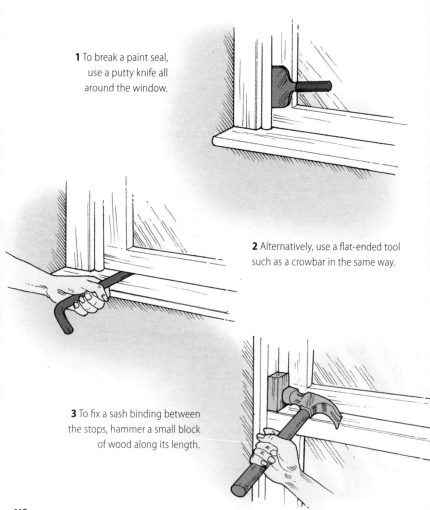

1 To break a paint seal, use a putty knife all around the window.

2 Alternatively, use a flat-ended tool such as a crowbar in the same way.

3 To fix a sash binding between the stops, hammer a small block of wood along its length.

REPLACING A DAMAGED SCREEN

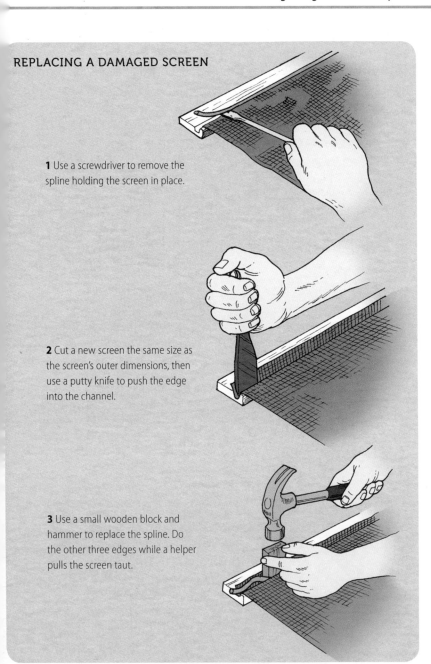

1 Use a screwdriver to remove the spline holding the screen in place.

2 Cut a new screen the same size as the screen's outer dimensions, then use a putty knife to push the edge into the channel.

3 Use a small wooden block and hammer to replace the spline. Do the other three edges while a helper pulls the screen taut.

LIGHT FITTINGS

Light on the subject Neglected light fittings and lampshades collect dust and grease, reducing the efficiency of light bulbs and tubes. Make sure you switch off the power before cleaning light fittings.

CHANDELIERS

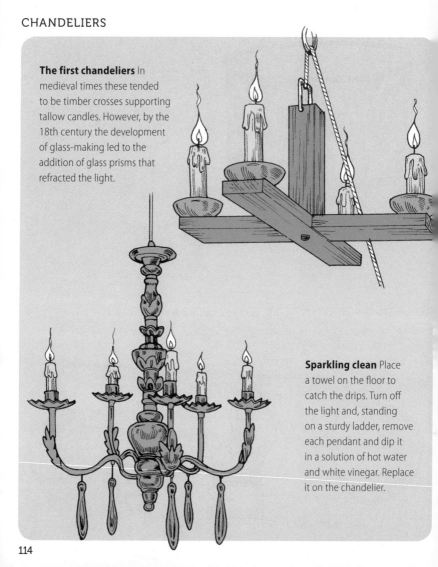

The first chandeliers In medieval times these tended to be timber crosses supporting tallow candles. However, by the 18th century the development of glass-making led to the addition of glass prisms that refracted the light.

Sparkling clean Place a towel on the floor to catch the drips. Turn off the light and, standing on a sturdy ladder, remove each pendant and dip it in a solution of hot water and white vinegar. Replace it on the chandelier.

AMPSHADES

Fabric, raffia and straw Vacuum with the upholstery brush attachment, but clean parchment with cotton buds and oatmeal.

REPLACING A BROKEN BULB WITH A SCREW-IN FITTING

1 Turn off the power at the main switch, then slice a potato in half.

2 Wearing gloves, use a pair of pliers to remove as much glass from the bulb as you can.

3 Press the cut side of the potato into the base of the bulb and unscrew it.

FIREPLACES

Home fires Regularly cleaning and maintaining your fireplace, whether it's behind a glass screen or in an open hearth, will provide your home with a safer, more efficient fire.

CLEANING AND MAINTENANCE

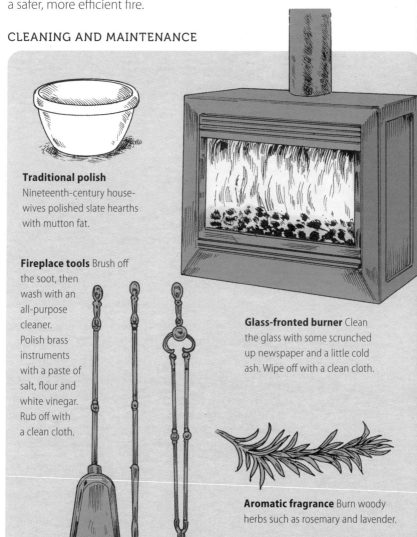

Traditional polish
Nineteenth-century house-wives polished slate hearths with mutton fat.

Fireplace tools Brush off the soot, then wash with an all-purpose cleaner. Polish brass instruments with a paste of salt, flour and white vinegar. Rub off with a clean cloth.

Glass-fronted burner Clean the glass with some scrunched up newspaper and a little cold ash. Wipe off with a clean cloth.

Aromatic fragrance Burn woody herbs such as rosemary and lavender.

Chimney sweep Hire a professional to do this once a year – a build-up of soot and creosote can result in a house fire.

Salty trick Reduce the amount of soot produced by a fire by throwing salt on the burning logs.

Open fireplace To subdue ashes when cleaning, use a spray bottle of water to cover them with a light mist. Sweep the hearth and vacuum any loose debris remaining, then wash the fireplace surround with a cleaner that's suitable for the surface – timber, ceramic or marble.

MIRRORS

Looking glass Mirrors are more than just a means of checking that your tie is on straight or your make-up is perfect – they can also reflect light or a pleasing view, making a room seem larger than it really is.

HANGING A MIRROR ON A PLASTERBOARD WALL

1 Find the structural timber or studs by knocking the wall, or use a stud finder.

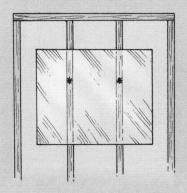

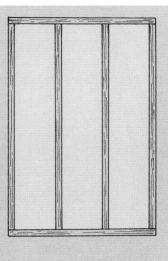

2 For a rectangular mirror you'll need to secure 2 hanging devices to the wall, positioned as above.

3 If you can secure the mirror to a stud wall, use 2 wall mates like this one.

4 If you have to secure the mirror to plasterboard, use 2 toggle mates – as you push each one through the wall, its wings will collapse, then reopen.

5 Hang the mirror with picture wire twisted around 2 screw eyes secured to the frame.

LEANING MIRROR GLASS

Stains Try rubbing stains with a paste of water and borax or bicarbonate of soda.

Polish Rub it with a clean cloth and a few drops of eucalytpus oil, which may help to stop the mirror from fogging. Or polish it with a ball of damp newspaper, followed by a ball of dry newspaper.

COMPUTERS

Home office If you have a computer at home, chances are the members of your household spend hours using it each day, so it's important to position the monitor and an adjustable chair in order to prevent repetitive strain injury

CLEANING THE COMPUTER

Screen
Always follow the manufacturer's advice on cleaning.

Keyboard Turn it upside down and shake it. Use a self-adhesive note to pick up dust. Wipe off marks with a damp cloth.

SETTING UP AN ERGONOMIC DESK

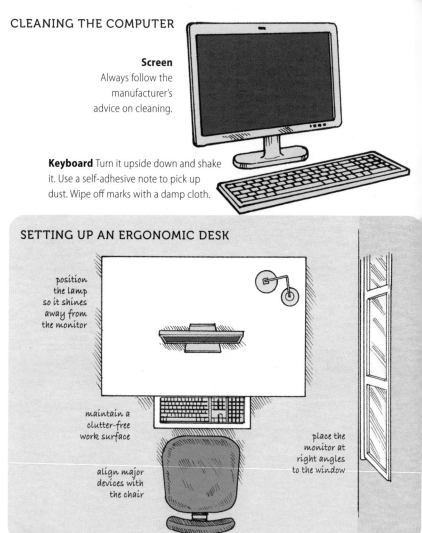

position the lamp so it shines away from the monitor

maintain a clutter-free work surface

align major devices with the chair

place the monitor at right angles to the window

MAINTAINING A GOOD POSTURE

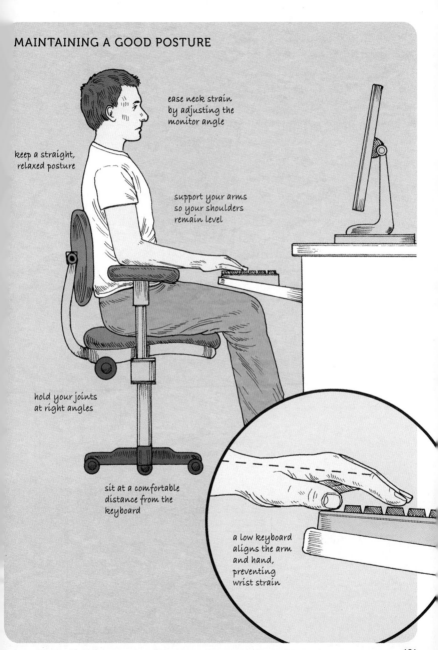

ease neck strain by adjusting the monitor angle

keep a straight, relaxed posture

support your arms so your shoulders remain level

hold your joints at right angles

sit at a comfortable distance from the keyboard

a low keyboard aligns the arm and hand, preventing wrist strain

THE KITCHEN

The enticing smell of baking, a pantry full of preserves and fresh fruit, vegetables and herbs from the kitchen garden can all be found in the heart of the home – the kitchen.

Is it fresh?

Food safety Not all produce has a use-by date to guide you, so here are some tips on how to tell if meat, seafood, dairy products, fruit, vegetables and grocery items are fresh, untainted and safe to eat.

MEAT AND CHICKEN

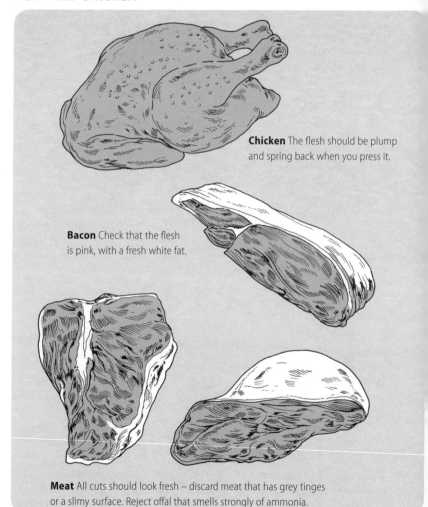

Chicken The flesh should be plump and spring back when you press it.

Bacon Check that the flesh is pink, with a fresh white fat.

Meat All cuts should look fresh – discard meat that has grey tinges or a slimy surface. Reject offal that smells strongly of ammonia.

EAFOOD

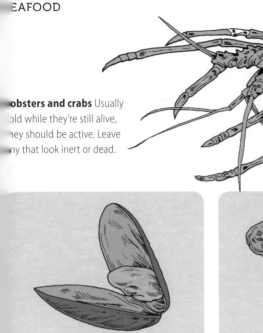

Lobsters and crabs Usually sold while they're still alive, they should be active. Leave any that look inert or dead.

Clams and mussels Dead molluscs won't open once they're cooked, so discard any that remain tightly shut.

Oysters Fresh oysters should be moist and plump with a fresh smell, and should close when they are tapped.

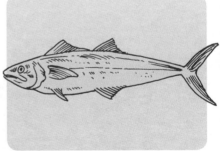

Prawns Whether fresh or cooked, prawns should be plump with a firm head. Discard any that are mushy or have a black head.

Fish The eyes should be clear and bulging, the gills a rich red and the skin plump. If pressing the skin with your finger leaves a dent, don't buy it.

EGGS AND DAIRY FOODS

Insulated bag Keep perishables in a cooler bag with a few frozen 'bricks' until you can get home and unpack the shopping.

Milk If you're not sure if it's fresh, pour a little into a cup of boiling water – if it curdles and separates, then it's off.

Eggs If an egg submerged in a pan of water floats, discard it.

Cheese Once it develops a lot of mould, discard it. If there's only a little, trim it off.

Yogurt If the curds have separated, don't eat it.

FRUIT AND VEGETABLES

press avocado gently near the stem – if it's soft, it's ripe

shake watermelons – they should rattle

avoid potatoes with shoots or green spots

buy corn with a bright green husk

check pineapples for a fragrant aroma

NON-PERISHABLES

packaging should be intact

check the use-by date on processed goods

avoid dairy products such as yogurt with swollen lids

don't buy frozen foods with clumps of ice attached – they may have been refrozen

dairy products should be cold

reject cans that are swollen, dented or rusty

How long will it keep?

Refrigerated items If you use drinks and food items within the recommended times, you may manage to avoid harbouring clumps of wizened vegetables and mouldy cheese in the back of the fridge.

cake, opened wine, fish and cooked chicken

milk, most vegetables, beef, herbs, pome fruit, berries and stone fruit

butter, eggs, sausages, ham, citrus, root vegetables and cheese

M	T	W	T	F	S	S
1	2	3	4	5	6	7
8	✗	✗	11	12	13	14
15	16	17	18	19	20	21
22	23	24	25	26	27	28
29	30	31				

M	T	W	T	F	S	S
1	2	3	4	5	6	7
8	✗	✗	✗	✗	✗	14
15	16	17	18	19	20	21
22	23	24	25	26	27	28
29	30	31				

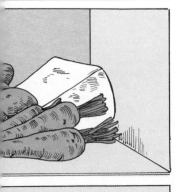

M	T	W	T	F	S	S
1	2	3	4	5	6	7
✗	✗	✗	✗	✗	✗	✗
✗	✗	✗	✗	✗	✗	✗
22	23	24	25	26	27	28
29	30	31				

FRIDGE HYGIENE

Safe storage There's more to storing food in the fridge than just placing ___ on a shelf and shutting the door. Some foods are prone to tainting and mus___ be covered while many others can be frozen only for a relatively short perio___

ICE CHEST

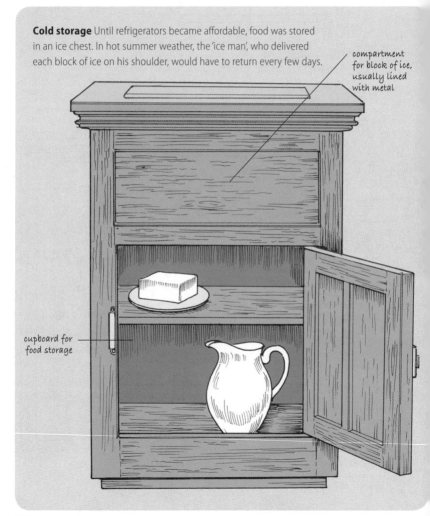

Cold storage Until refrigerators became affordable, food was stored in an ice chest. In hot summer weather, the 'ice man', who delivered each block of ice on his shoulder, would have to return every few days.

compartment for block of ice, usually lined with metal

cupboard for food storage

REFRIGERATOR

The organised fridge If you remove plastic packaging from fresh produce as soon as you bring it home, and store it correctly, it will last longer. Try to clean out your fridge once a week.

keep frozen beef and poultry for up to one year

store frozen vegetables for up to one year

store eggs in their carton

keep butter covered to prevent tainting

place fish on a plate and cover it with plastic wrap

unwrap meat and put it in a pudding bowl topped with a plate

store vegetables in the crisper

How to cut exotic fruit

Fruits of the sun Many tropical fruits have a big seed, or protect their flesh with a tough skin or shell, so it's useful to know the correct techniques for cutting and preparing these delicious fruits when they are fully ripe.

DISLODGING POMEGRANATE ARILS

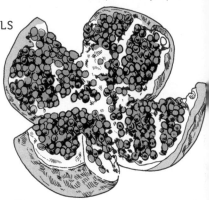

Fruity flower Slice the top off at the stem end, then cut it into four sections so it opens out like a flower. Hold it upside down over a bowl and whack it with a wooden spoon.

CRACKING A COCONUT

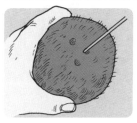

1 Use a nail to score dents in two of the soft spots, or eyes.

2 With a hammer, drive the nail into the two spots.

3 Turn the coconut upside down and drain the milk.

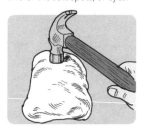

4 Wrap the coconut in an old towel and hammer it until it breaks down into chunks.

5 Using a sharp knife, carefully remove the flesh from the husk. This will take a while.

6 Cut off the inner shell and store chunks in water in the fridge. Change the water daily.

CUTTING A MANGO HEDGEHOG

1 Slice off both 'cheeks', avoiding the pith.

2 Cut across the flesh of each cheek at right angles.

3 Turn the cheek inside out so the pieces are easy to eat.

SLICING A PINEAPPLE

1 Cut off the top and bottom of the pineapple.

2 Slice off the rind in several sections around the fruit.

3 Slice the fruit and remove the hard core.

PITTING AN AVOCADO

1 Cut the avocado in half and twist it apart.

2 Separate the halves. The pit will be in one of the halves.

3 Tap the knife so it grips the pit, then remove it.

THE PANTRY

The efficient kitchen A well-organised pantry, stocked with staples, will not only make it easier to prepare last-minute meals and draw up your shopping list but will also cut down on waste, thus saving you money.

ORGANISING TIPS

file herbs and spices alphabetically in a CD box

keep loose recipes in a binder

use chalk on blackboard paint to label jars

keep like things together – for example, keep condiments in a tray

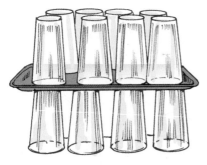

create an extra shelf with a tray

put cans and jars on a lazy susan

PANTRY STAPLES

Baking products Baking powder, bicarbonate of soda, breadcrumbs, cornflour, flour (self-raising, plain), sugars (brown, white, caster, icing), yeast

Beverages Coffee, tea, cocoa powder

Cans Beans, coconut milk, tomatoes

Condiments Salt, pepper, mustards, sauces (soy, Worcestershire, tabasco)

Dried fruit and nuts

Dried herbs and spices

Dried pulses Beans (borlotti, broad, cannellini), chickpeas, lentils

Grains Cereals, couscous, noodles, pasta, polenta, rice (long-grain, short-grain, arborio), rolled oats, semolina

Oils Olive, sesame, vegetable

Spreads Honey, jams, peanut butter

Stocks Chicken, meat, vegetable

Vinegars Brown, balsamic, red wine, white, white wine

IDEAS FOR SAVING MONEY

Hidden persuaders Supermarket designers have refined several techniques to make you slow down and buy more than you intended. Here are some ideas for cutting your shopping costs.

PLAN AHEAD

Plan your meals Make a shopping list and stick to it.

Buy in bulk Buy non-perishables such as soap and toilet paper in bulk.

Bargains Look for items that are on sale.

SALE

Buy wholesale Cut a rack of lamb into chops.

Make your own Don't buy commercial cleaning products.

Comparison shop Use a calculator to check the price per gram or litre.

AVOID PROCESSED PRODUCTS

Soft drinks Make them with fruit juice.

FRUIT JUICE + SODA WATER = CARBONATED FRUIT JUICE

CUT OUT THE 'MIDDLE MAN'

Bake your own Make bread, cakes, biscuits and muesli bars from quality ingredients.

Buy direct Join a fruit and vegetable co-op, or shop at a farmers' market.

Grow your own herbs Pick fresh herbs as you need them.

BE A 'GREEN' SHOPPER

Tread lightly 'Green' shopping involves avoiding buying over-packaged goods and many plastic items and purchasing fresh, whole organic food as well as products manufactured under fair trade agreements.

PLASTIC PRODUCTS

avoid buying disposable plastic plates, cups and cutlery

use reusable shopping bags

don't buy disposable nappies

buy biodegradable bin liners

unless it is unsafe to drink tap water, avoid bottled water

use refillable containers for products such as honey

UY FREE-RANGE EGGS AND CHICKENS

FAIR TRADE PRODUCTS

Ethical shopping If you're buying items made in developing countries, check that they were made with sustainable materials for fair wages.

COFFEE

Takeaway cup If you regularly buy takeaway coffee, use your own insulated cup with its own lid.

Organic coffee Coffee crops are sprayed with fungicides, and processing instant coffee uses a lot of energy. Buy organic ground coffee or beans.

Cooking tips

Basic skills Here's a collection of handy tips as well as recipes and simple instructions for making your own pizza and pasta – both perennial favourites with all ages.

USEFUL HINTS

Ripen an avocado Place it in a brown paper bag with a ripe apple or banana.

Remove almond skins Soak in boiling water for a few minutes, then plunge in cold water.

Protect the pot To stop artichokes from turning an aluminium pot grey, first soak them in water with 1 tablespoon vinegar.

Anchovies too salty? Soak them in milk for 10 minutes.

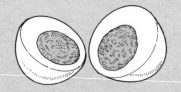

Stop an egg cracking Use a needle to prick a hole in the blunt end.

Rosemary skewers
Strip most of the foliage,
leaving some at one end.

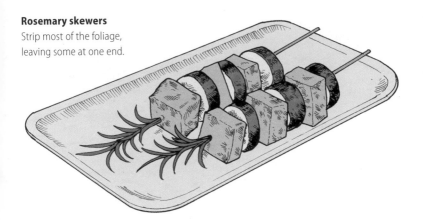

Tearless onions Before
chopping onions, chill them
in the freezer for 10 minutes.

Peeled orange Cover it with
boiling water and the pith and
peel will come away cleanly.

Peeled beetroot Put cooked
beetroot in a bowl of cold
water before peeling.

Spreadable butter To soften
cold butter, beat in a few drops
of boiling water.

Extra flavour To enhance the
flavour of mint, chop it with a
little caster sugar.

White cauliflower curds
Add some lemon peel to the
cooking water.

MAKING PASTA

1 To a well in 280 g flour, add 4 egg yolks and 2 teaspoons olive oil, beaten together.

2 Use a fork to draw in the flour.

3 Roll the dough into a ball.

4 Knead on a floured board.

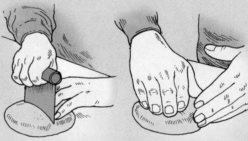

5 Divide into quarters.

6 Flatten each into a disc.

7 Roll out the dough.

8 Flip and roll again.

9 Check for transparency.

CUTTING FETTUCINE

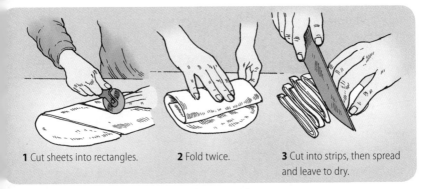

1 Cut sheets into rectangles.

2 Fold twice.

3 Cut into strips, then spread and leave to dry.

MAKING TORTELLINI

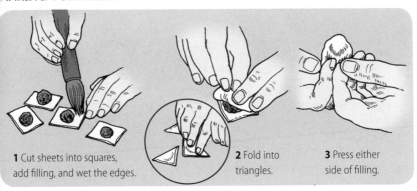

1 Cut sheets into squares, add filling, and wet the edges.

2 Fold into triangles.

3 Press either side of filling.

IDENTIFYING PASTA SHAPES

farfalle

spirali

penne

MAKING PIZZA

Personalised pizza Experiment
with toppings, using vegetables
and herbs that you have
grown yourself.

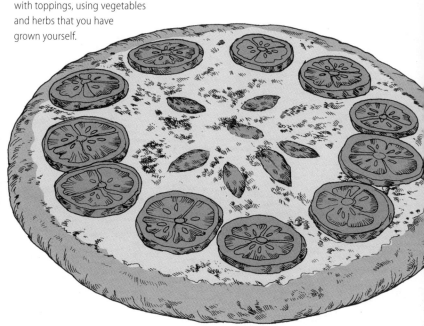

Handy tools Invest in a pizza stone,
which helps the bottom
to cook faster,
and a cutter.

Pizza dough
* 400 g plain flour
* 1 tablespoon dried yeast
* 1 teaspoon salt
* 1 tablespoon olive oil
* 1 cup lukewarm water

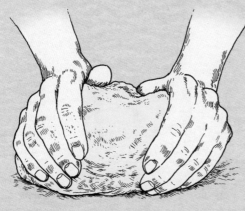

1 Mix together dry ingredients. Mix together oil and water and mix into dry ingredients. Knead until dough is smooth and elastic.

2 Transfer dough into bowl greased with a little oil. Cover with clean towel and leave until it has doubled in size. Knock it back, divide into 2 or 3 portions, cover, then leave to rise again.

3 Roll out each on a floured board, then add desired toppings. Serves 4.

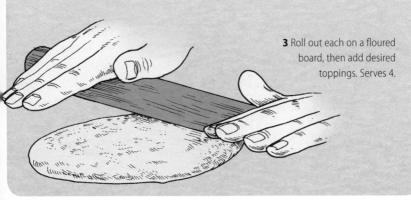

Afternoon Tea

Baking day In our grandmothers' day, baking day was a weekly event. There are still few things more inviting than the smell of freshly baked bread, just out of the oven, or the sight of a lavishly iced and decorated cake.

CELEBRATION CAKES

Natural colouring Soak a few coffee berries in 1 egg white until it turns green.

Candle wax To protect the cake, stand the candles in marshmallows.

Quick-setting icing Add a little vinegar to the mixture.

Chocolate cake Dust the greased cake tin with coco powder instead of flour.

Sugar nippers Until the 19th century, sugar was sold in hard 'loaves' that had to be cut with special tools.

BAKING TIPS

Lighter scones Use hot milk instead of cold.

Chocolate curls Melt 100 g chocolate in a bowl over a pan of simmering water. Pour onto a marble slab, cool. Push a knife across the surface.

Floral decoration Paint violets with beaten egg white, then dip in caster sugar. Leave 12 hours to dry.

Out of self-raising flour? To 1 cup plain flour add 1½ teaspoons baking powder.

Communal oven Have a bread-baking day with friends, using the same oven. Mark each loaf with a different design so you can identify the baker.

147

Kitchen economy

Waste not We tend to throw out phenomenal quantities of good food rather than eat leftovers or reuse them in a creative way, but there are lots of easy ways to make the most of leftovers as well as food past its best.

USING WHAT YOU HAVE

Over-ripe bananas Use them to make smoothies and banana bread.

French toast Dip stale bread in beaten egg and milk, then fry in butter until golden. Sprinkle with cinnamon and sugar.

Vegetable soup Make a stock from a chicken carcass and vegetable trimmings, then sauté 1 clove garlic and 1 small onion in 2 tablespoons olive oil. Add chopped vegetables, 1 tin peeled tomatoes and 1 litre stock. Cook until vegetables are tender and season to taste. Serves 4.

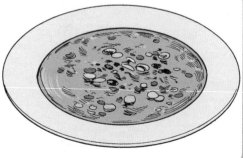

Fried rice This is a great way to use leftover rice and bits of vegetables.

Sandwiches Make sandwiches and wraps with leftover meat and chicken.

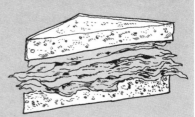

Omelette Turn stumps of cheese, a few eggs and some vegetables into an omelette.

Handy bags Use zip-lock bags to freeze leftover egg whites, coconut milk and wine.

Potato croquettes Use up leftover vegetables and mashed potato.

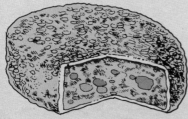

Save the zest When squeezing citrus juice, pare the zest and store it in an airtight container in the freezer.

Kitchen garden

Grow your own Even if you live in an apartment, you may be able to grow a pot of herbs on a sunny windowsill, or train an espaliered citrus tree against a balcony wall. If you have room, try this simple veggie garden plan.

'SQUARE FOOT' SUMMER GARDENING PLAN

Crop rotation To avoid encouraging pests and diseases, at the end of each season rotate each crop so nothing grows in the same square two seasons in a row.

grow peas and beans against a wall or some other form of support

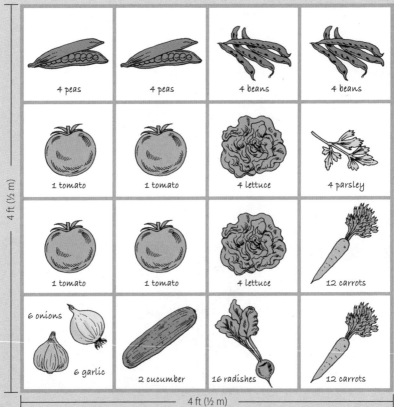

4 peas	4 peas	4 beans	4 beans
1 tomato	1 tomato	4 lettuce	4 parsley
1 tomato	1 tomato	4 lettuce	12 carrots
6 onions / 6 garlic	2 cucumber	16 radishes	12 carrots

4 ft (½ m)

4 ft (½ m)

TRAINING FRUIT TREES AGAINST A WALL

Ancient pruning technique

There are several advantages to growing a two-dimensional fruit tree: it takes up less space; it can hide an ugly wall; when planted next to a wall, the radiant heat emitted by the wall overnight can help extend the growing season; and it makes the fruit easier to reach.

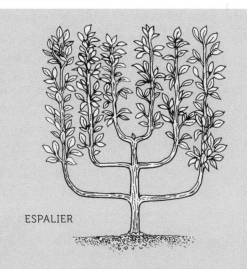

ESPALIER

CORDON

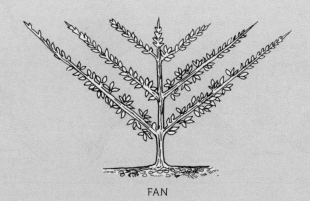

FAN

EDIBLE ORNAMENTALS

sunflower

strawberry

kale

artichoke

grapes

'Romanesco' broccoli

ROWING HERBS IN A COLD CLIMATE

Sunny spot Install glass shelves in a sunny window, or arrange the pots on the sill.

PROLONGING THE HARVEST

Best quality Herbs, fruit and vegetables require various storing methods, although pome fruit and root vegetables will store for a much longer period. Follow these guidelines for keeping healthy produce fit for eating.

DRYING AND STORING

Dried herbs
Hang bunches in a cool, dry place.

TRADITIONAL STORAGE

Vegetable clamp or 'pie'
Store only sound vegetables in this insulated mound, which keeps out light, frost and pests.

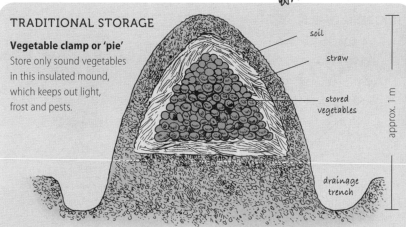

soil

straw

stored vegetables

approx. 1 m

drainage trench

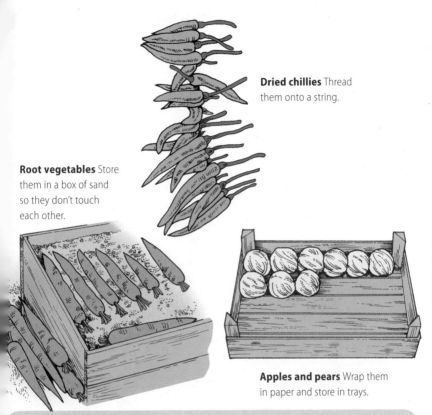

Dried chillies Thread them onto a string.

Root vegetables Store them in a box of sand so they don't touch each other.

Apples and pears Wrap them in paper and store in trays.

PLAITING GARLIC

1 Tie together 4 plants that have been dried in the sun for several days.

2 Position 2 more plants, one to each side and start plaiting. Add one to the middle.

3 Keep going in this way, plaiting together all the plant stems.

Kitchen garden gluts

Harvest of plenty If you have more fresh produce than you can use, consider these ideas for freezing, preserving and drying, or use them in jams, butters, drinks, soups, chutneys, relishes and sauces.

CITRUS

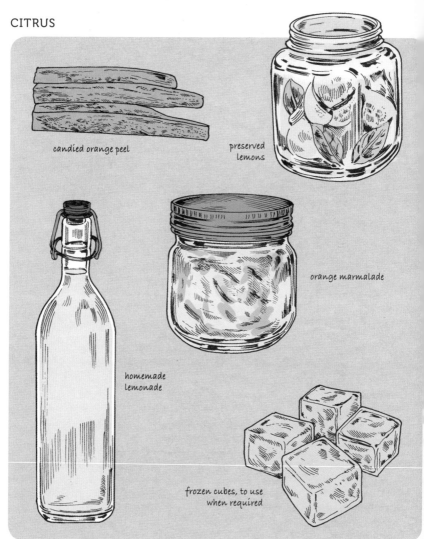

candied orange peel

preserved lemons

orange marmalade

homemade lemonade

frozen cubes, to use when required

ERBS

herb butter

frozen
chopped
herbs

bouquet garni (bay,
thyme, parsley
and rosemary)

Basil pesto

✳ 1½ cups basil leaves
✳ ¼ cup toasted pine nuts
✳ ¾ cup grated parmesan
✳ 5 tablespoons olive oil

1 Process first 3 ingredients until smooth.
2 Add oil in a thin stream until smooth.
3 Decant into a sterilised jar, cover with
olive oil and freeze.

ROASTING CAPSICUM

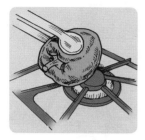

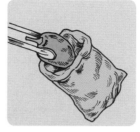

1 Use a pair of tongs to hold it over a flame. Keep turning the fruit until the skin is black.

2 Place it in a brown paper bag. This will generate enough steam to loosen the skin.

3 Peel off the skin. Slice the fruit and place it in a jar, cover with olive oil and seal.

TOMATO DISHES

tomato soup

tomato bruschetta

PEELING TOMATOES

1 Score a cross in the base of each tomato, then place in hot water for 30 seconds.

2 Transfer the tomatoes to a bowl of iced water and let them stand for 5 minutes.

3 Remove, then peel back from the scored cuts. Use immediately or freeze.

Passata

* 1 kg ripe 'Roma' tomatoes, washed and halved
* 1 small onion, chopped
* 2 tablespoons olive oil

1 Cook tomatoes in large saucepan over medium heat for 10 minutes.

2 Purée, then pass through a sieve or passata machine. Discard seeds and skin.

3 Sauté onion in oil over low heat. Add tomatoes and cook, stirring for 30 minutes.

4 Bottle, store in fridge for 1 week or freeze for 3 months.

Other ideas Make some tomato relish, chutney or tomato sauce.

OVEN-DRIED TOMATOES

1 Cut 'Roma' tomatoes in half and place them on baking paper on a tray.

2 Sprinkle with salt and herbs to taste, then bake in the oven at lowest temperature for up to 8 hours.

3 Store in sterilised jars, cover with olive oil and seal.

Kitchen pests

Organic control The first line of defence is to always keep your kitchen scrupulously clean, as food debris attracts pests. The second is to try a range of non-chemical strategies that will deter or harm only the pests.

COCKROACHES

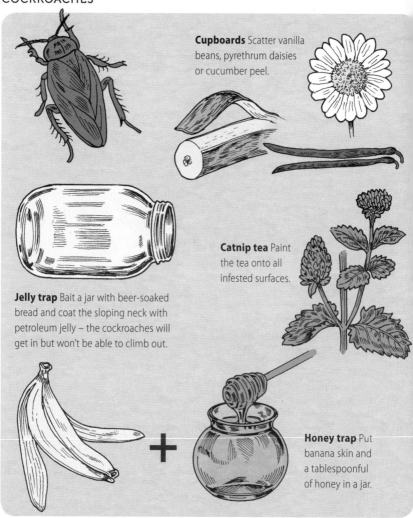

Cupboards Scatter vanilla beans, pyrethrum daisies or cucumber peel.

Catnip tea Paint the tea onto all infested surfaces.

Jelly trap Bait a jar with beer-soaked bread and coat the sloping neck with petroleum jelly – the cockroaches will get in but won't be able to climb out.

Honey trap Put banana skin and a tablespoonful of honey in a jar.

FLIES

fly swat

1 Mix together ¼ cup golden or maple syrup and 1 teaspoon each of brown and white sugar.

2 Soak strips of brown paper in the syrup overnight, then hang to dry.

ANTS

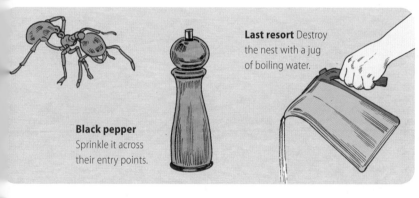

Last resort Destroy the nest with a jug of boiling water.

Black pepper Sprinkle it across their entry points.

RODENTS

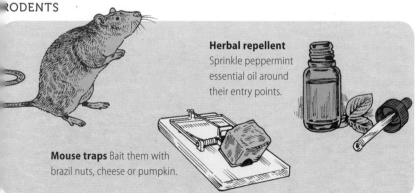

Herbal repellent Sprinkle peppermint essential oil around their entry points.

Mouse traps Bait them with brazil nuts, cheese or pumpkin.

CLEANING TASKS

Old-fashioned tips There's no need to fall back on chemical cleaning products just to keep cook- and bakeware clean. Wipe down your cooktop each time you use it, and follow these simple cleaning tips.

ROUTINE JOBS

Burnt pie dish Dip it in very hot water, then turn it upside down on newspaper so the steam can loosen the remnants.

Season bakeware After washing, use a paper towel to wipe over a little vegetable or olive oil.

Tea stains Fill the teapot with a solution of 1 part salt to 2 parts water. Leave overnight, then rinse.

Dirty cooktop Leave cloths, which have been soaked in hot water, on the cooktop overnight. Clean away the residue the next morning.

Meatscreens Cooks in the 18th century used these to cook meat in front of an open fire, checking its progress through the door at the back.

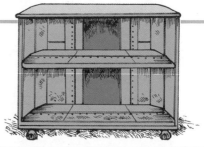

ERUSTING A CAST IRON PAN

1 Rub the rust with a pad of steel wool.

2 Coat the pan with oil and add enough salt to create a paste.

3 Scrub with some paper towels, then rinse.

LEANING POTS AND PANS

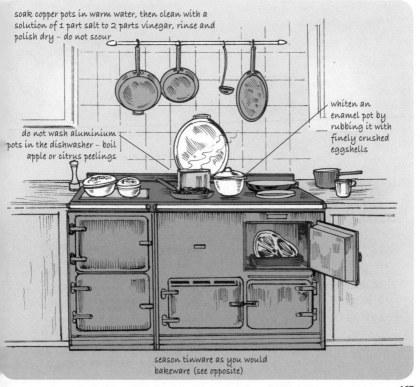

soak copper pots in warm water, then clean with a solution of 1 part salt to 2 parts vinegar, rinse and polish dry – do not scour

do not wash aluminium pots in the dishwasher – boil apple or citrus peelings

whiten an enamel pot by rubbing it with finely crushed eggshells

season tinware as you would bakeware (see opposite)

WINE

One of life's joys Even if your wine stocks are modest, you should take care to prevent your wine from deteriorating. The main requirements are cc temperatures, low light and enough humidity to stop the cork drying out.

STORING WINE

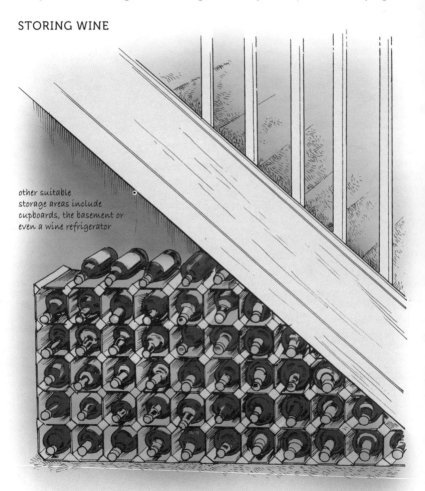

other suitable storage areas include cupboards, the basement or even a wine refrigerator

Ideal conditions Store wine in a cool, dark place at a stable temperature, ideally 5–18°C. Lay down any bottles with corks so the cork remains moist.

WINE SAVER

Vacuum pump If you don't finish a bottle of wine, pump out all the air and cork it with a stopper.

UNCORKING A BOTTLE OF WINE

1 Cut the foil seal and remove it.

2 Twist the corkscrew halfway into the cork.

3 Place the lever on the rim and pull.

POURING WINE WHEN THE CORK IS BROKEN

1 Push the cork back with a straw, then pour wine into a coffee filter placed in a glass.

2 Let the wine drain into the glass.

3 Remove the filter.

THE LINEN PRESS

Every household needs a neat, well-organised linen press so it's easy to find tea towels, bed and table linen, blankets and duvets when you need them.

ABOUT THE LINEN PRESS

Wrinkle remover The term 'press' derives from the fact that a few thousand years ago, a simple mechanism was used to literally press out wrinkles. Now it's more likely to be a specially designed built-in cupboard.

SCREW PRESS, C. 1850

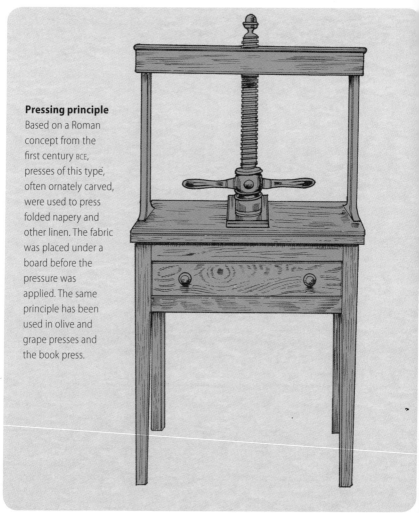

Pressing principle
Based on a Roman concept from the first century BCE, presses of this type, often ornately carved, were used to press folded napery and other linen. The fabric was placed under a board before the pressure was applied. The same principle has been used in olive and grape presses and the book press.

EORGIAN LINEN PRESS, 18TH CENTURY

Status symbol A linen press could also be a handsome cupboard, which in effect boasted the household's suppy of linen, once considered an indicator of wealth. And if you owned plenty of linen, you could last until the next 'great wash'.

STORAGE PRINCIPLES

Save time and energy All members of the household have access to the linen press, so it makes sense to have a well-organised cupboard full of clean linen and bedding. Store the items you use most at eye level.

GENERAL TIPS

* Store bulky items such as blankets and doonas on the higher shelves.
* Put towels together, table linen together.
* Spread the wear by placing freshly laundered linen on the bottom of the pile and using items from the top.
* Add baskets and boxes to make your storage more flexible.
* Line the shelves in case unfinished timber damages the linen.
* Add an open box of chalk to help absorb damp.

DO'S AND DON'TS

Do add a bar of scented soap to each shelf – it will also last longer once you use it.

Do use sachets of dried lavender, cloves, feverfew, peppermint, eucalyptus, bay leaves or dried citrus peel to repel moths. Place the sachets in drawers, or hang them from coathangers.

Don't use cedar balls and blocks – they yellow and damage delicate linens.

Don't starch linen – starch attracts silverfish, which eat it, leaving a telltale stain.

Don't store dirty, damp items. Dirt will attract pests, and damp will encourage mildew.

3 IDEAS FOR STORING TABLECLOTHS

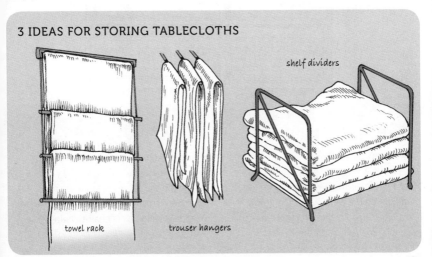

towel rack

trouser hangers

shelf dividers

BED LINEN

A clean sheet Although fitted sheets make bed-making much easier and quicker, folding them can present a challenge. Try to air the bed before you make it each day, and wash your bed linen once a week.

FOLDING A FITTED SHEET

1 With a short side facing you, fold it in half, tucking in the gathered corners.

2 Pull across one gathered corner and tuck it inside the other.

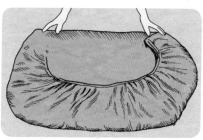

3 Smooth out the sheet.

4 Fold it in thirds lengthwise.

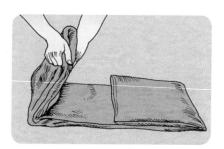

5 Fold in quarters from one short end.

6 Stack neatly in the linen press.

OLPROOF STORAGE

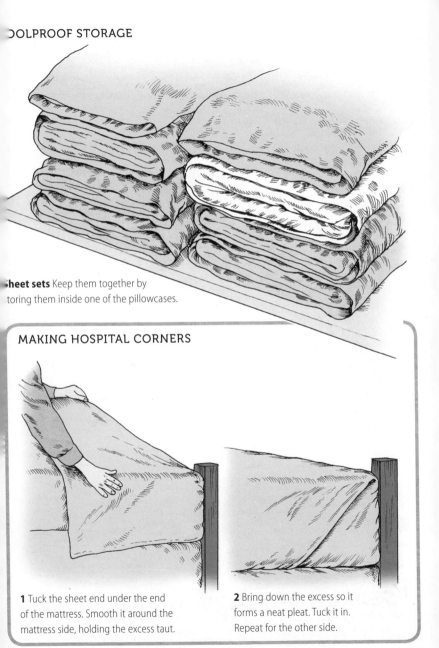

Sheet sets Keep them together by
storing them inside one of the pillowcases.

MAKING HOSPITAL CORNERS

1 Tuck the sheet end under the end
of the mattress. Smooth it around the
mattress side, holding the excess taut.

2 Bring down the excess so it
forms a neat pleat. Tuck it in.
Repeat for the other side.

Blankets

Warmth and comfort A good quality pure wool blanket will last a lifetime, but you can also choose other durable, sustainable fabrics, such as hemp and bamboo. Wash them regularly, and dry them in the sun.

ECO-FRIENDLY BLANKET CHOICES

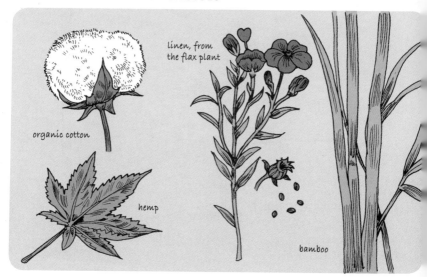

organic cotton

hemp

linen, from the flax plant

bamboo

BED WARMERS

Copper warming pan It has air holes to release the fumes from burning embers, coal or peat.

Scottish bed warmer Made of stoneware, the 'pig' is filled with hot water.

CARING FOR PURE WOOL

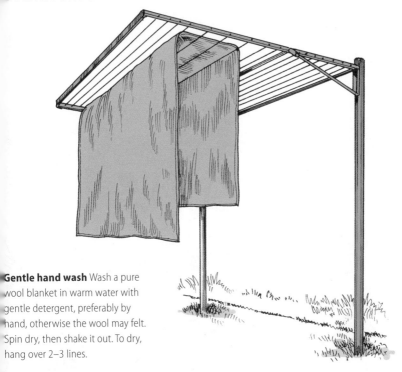

Gentle hand wash Wash a pure wool blanket in warm water with gentle detergent, preferably by hand, otherwise the wool may felt. Spin dry, then shake it out. To dry, hang over 2–3 lines.

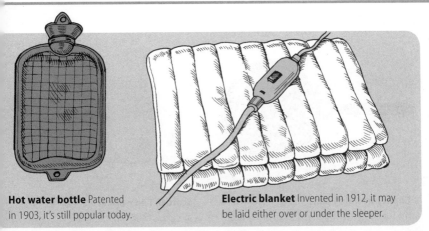

Hot water bottle Patented in 1903, it's still popular today.

Electric blanket Invented in 1912, it may be laid either over or under the sleeper.

DUVETS AND PILLOWS

Soft as a feather Duvets and pillows need to be regularly cleaned – especially if you suffer from allergies – but it is possible to avoid the expense of dry-cleaning by washing them yourself, at least once a year.

WASHING A DOWN DUVET

Stamp out the dirt
Fill the bath with warm water, add a little mild detergent and agitate the duvet by stomping on it. Rinse three times, squeeze out the excess water and spin dry. Do the same with down or feather pillows.

DRYING A DOWN DUVET

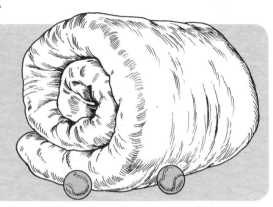

1 Hang the duvet on the clothesline to dry in the sun, and shake it out regularly to redistribute the down.

2 Dry it in a tumble dryer with two tennis balls, which will help fluff up the feathers.

FOR ALLERGY SUFFERERS

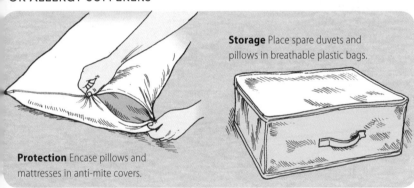

Storage Place spare duvets and pillows in breathable plastic bags.

Protection Encase pillows and mattresses in anti-mite covers.

DID YOU KNOW?

Eiderdown is a quilt filled with the down of the eider duck.

Ticking is a closely woven, often striped fabric designed to stop feathers poking out.

Towels and tea towels

Drying off A thick, soft, absorbent towel is one of life's little pleasures, while spotless tea towels can form part of your kitchen décor. Invest in the best quality you can afford and they'll reward you with years of service.

FOLDING TOWELS

1 Fold each towel in half lengthways.

2 Fold it into thirds.

3 Store all your matching sets together.

TEA TOWELS

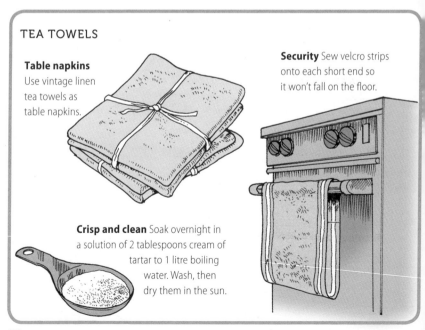

Table napkins Use vintage linen tea towels as table napkins.

Security Sew velcro strips onto each short end so it won't fall on the floor.

Crisp and clean Soak overnight in a solution of 2 tablespoons cream of tartar to 1 litre boiling water. Wash, then dry them in the sun.

5 IDEAS FOR REUSING ODD TOWELS

mismatched towels coordinated with the same trim

beach bag

bath mitts

hooded towel for a baby

hot water bottle cover

TABLE LINEN

Heirlooms If your linen press features embroidered table linen – perhaps worked by your mother or grandmother – it's well worth the effort to keep it free of stains so you can pass it on to the next generation.

REMOVING PROBLEM STAINS

Rust stains Rub in a paste of lemon juice and salt, leave for up to 20 minutes, then rinse out.

Lipstick Blot with a little ammonia, then use your fingertip to rub on a drop of dishwashing detergent. Rinse. If that doesn't work, try a commercial stain remover.

Candle wax Rub the wax with an ice cube, then peel off. Blot the residue with eucalyptus oil and wash.

Grease Place the fabric between 2 pieces of blotting paper and iron it.

Yellowing Soak overnight in a tub of water with 1 cup of cream of tartar, then launder as usual.

OLDING A ROUND TABLECLOTH

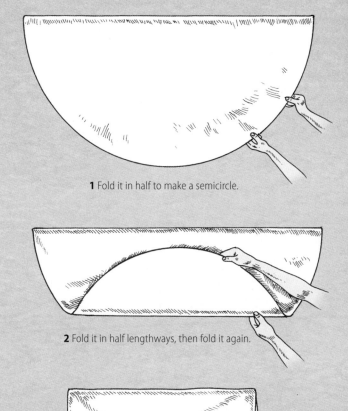

1 Fold it in half to make a semicircle.

2 Fold it in half lengthways, then fold it again.

3 From the short end, fold it in thirds or quarters.

Napkin Folding

Special occasion The art of napkin folding may seem a little retro, unless you're eating at a fine-dining establishment, but a set of crisp, clean damask or linen table napkins can add the perfect flourish to a formal table setting.

THE PYRAMID

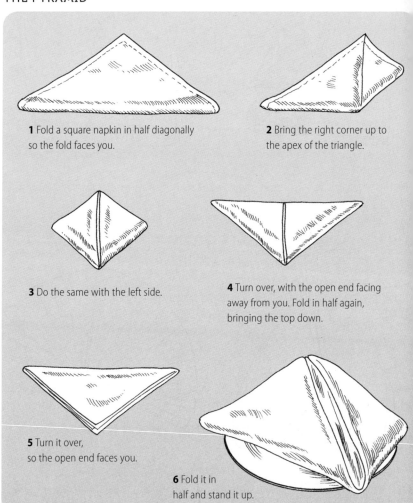

1 Fold a square napkin in half diagonally so the fold faces you.

2 Bring the right corner up to the apex of the triangle.

3 Do the same with the left side.

4 Turn over, with the open end facing away from you. Fold in half again, bringing the top down.

5 Turn it over, so the open end faces you.

6 Fold it in half and stand it up.

THE FAN

Fold in half lengthwise, and pleat the short side until there is one-third left.

2 Fold in half again, keeping all the pleats on the outside.

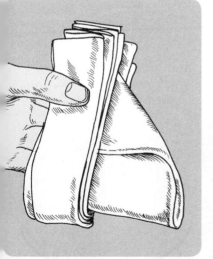

3 Fold in the top corner of the unfolded part diagonally, tucking it under the pleated folds.

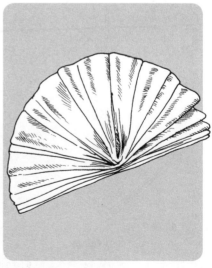

4 Open the fan and position the 'stand' so it faces away from the diner.

Past their best

A second life When sheets, blankets and tablecloths develop a hole or two or become frayed, you needn't throw them out. There are lots of ways to 'repurpose' the undamaged parts and use them in the house and garden.

4 IDEAS FOR REUSING OLD SHEETS

tunnel cloche for frost protection in the garden

laundry bag

drop sheet when painting and decorating

ghost costume

IDEAS FOR REUSING OLD BLANKETS

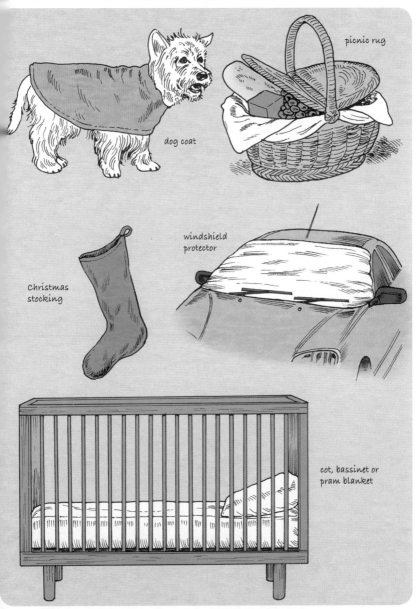

picnic rug

dog coat

Christmas stocking

windshield protector

cot, bassinet or pram blanket

5 IDEAS FOR REUSING OLD TABLECLOTHS

Simple projects If an old tablecloth holds great sentimental value for you, consider using the undamaged part in a patchwork quilt, or one of these projects.

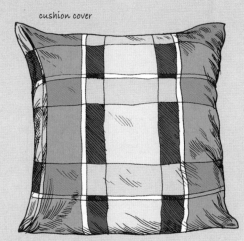

cushion cover

guest towels or
table napkins

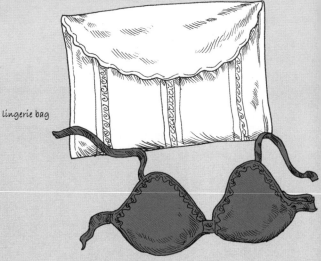

lingerie bag

lampshade

apron

WASHING AND IRONING

Washing day was once commonly performed on Mondays, so housewives and maids would have time to dry and press garments and linen by the following Sunday, the day of rest.

ORGANISING THE WASH

Extra care To make washing easier and more efficient, encourage the members of your household to sort their dirty clothes into the appropriate containers, and always read a new garment's care label before washing it.

SORTING THE WASH

Separate bins Keep whites, colours and delicates separate, then sort again into lightly soiled and heavily soiled.

CARE SYMBOLS

| cold machine wash | warm machine wash | hot machine wash | permanent press | delicate/ gentle |

...ASTENERS

Secure buttons To prevent buttons falling off in the wash, dab a little clear nail polish on the stitching.

Buttons and cuffs Undo buttons, as the agitation may cause buttonholes to tear, and unroll cuffs so they wash and dry properly.

Drawstrings Tie them so they don't get tangled around smaller items.

Zips Fasten them, as the zip teeth can damage clothing.

do not wash in water

hand wash

dry clean

bleach

do not bleach

WASHING TIPS

Edit the wash The convenience of modern washers and dryers makes it easy to wash garments after every wear, but sometimes all that's required is brief airing. Your clothes will last longer, and you'll save energy and water too.

HELPFUL HINTS

Non-colourfast garment Wash it alone with an old white sock until it stops releasing dye.

Black garments To minimise fading, turn them inside out before washing.

Gym gear Wash exercise clothes as soon as you get home, according to label directions.

Sleepwear Wash pyjamas and nighties at least as often as you do your sheets – once a week.

Tired of losing socks? Pin them together before the wash.

Empty the pockets Always check pockets for coins, tissues and other small items.

Denim If you wash jeans too often, the colour will fade.

Does it need washing? If a garment has been worn only once, simply air it.

Bed linen If you are prone to dermatitis, remove the fabric finishes by washing bed linen before using it.

Removing stains

Immediate action The golden rule is to remove stains as soon as you can. Always work from the outside of a stain so you don't spread it, and use a blunt knife or spatula to remove any solids.

ELBOW GREASE

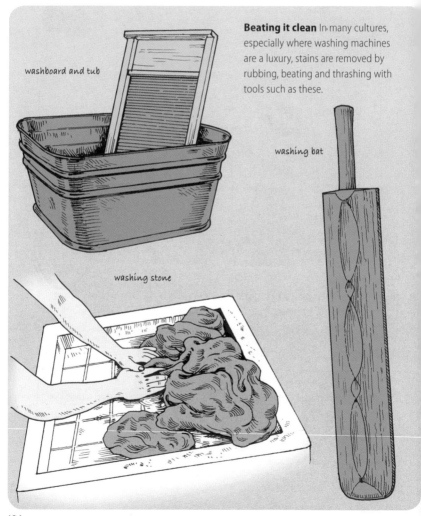

washboard and tub

Beating it clean In many cultures, especially where washing machines are a luxury, stains are removed by rubbing, beating and thrashing with tools such as these.

washing bat

washing stone

REMOVING COMMON STAINS

Tomato Soak the stain in white vinegar.

Berries Rub the stains with a piece of raw potato. For stubborn marks, dip the cut potato in lemon juice.

Lipstick Soak in white vinegar.

Blood Apply a paste of equal parts cold water and cornflour.

Red wine Stretch fabric over a bowl, cover with salt, then carefully pour boiling water over it from a height of about 40 cm.

Ink Soak in white vinegar or milk.

Scorch mark Soak the mark in lemon juice for half an hour. Rinse in warm water and dry in the sun.

WASHING WHITES

Nature's help Modern householders tend to underestimate the value of relying on nature to brighten whites – why not try leaving a yellowing or dull item in the sun for a few days?

TRADITIONAL METHODS

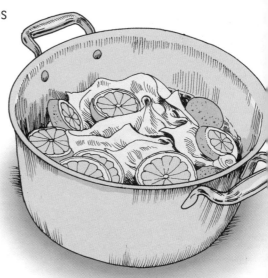

Borax Add ½ cup of borax to a washing load, but note the water must be hot – at least 60°C.

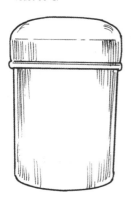

Lemon Fill a big pot with water, add several slices of lemon and bring to the boil. Remove from the heat, soak items to be whitened for up to an hour, then wash as usual.

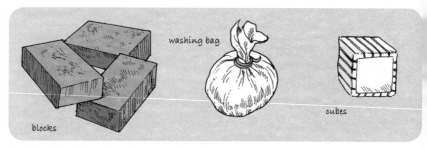

blocks

washing bag

cubes

Washing blue Use washing blue, made from the pigment indigo or smalt (powdered glass and cobalt), in the final rinse. It gives the optical illusion of whitening whites by disguising the yellow.

BLEACHING GREEN

Sun-whitened linen One traditional method for brightening whites was to lay it out on the grass or on a hedge, in the sun.

Starching

Adding body to clothes and linen You can buy commercial starch sprays, but it's safer and cheaper to make your own vegetable starches. Some can be used in the wash while others can be sprayed on while ironing.

MAKING POTATO STARCH

1 Peel 4 large potatoes.

2 Grate them, add them to a pot and cover with water. Mix it around a little, and leave to soak for 2 hours.

3 Mix again. Strain the solids through a sieve and drain off the water. Store in the fridge. See also step 2 below.

MAKING RICE STARCH

1 Boil ½ cup rice in ½ litre water until the rice is soft enough to mash by hand. Strain it and store the liquid in the fridge, shaking it occasionally.

2 Dip the garment into the starch water after washing and rinsing, then squeeze out any excess water. Hang it up to dry but iron it while it is still slightly damp.

RILLS AND FLOUNCES

Fine linen Through the centuries, whenever stiff lace collars and petticoats were in fashion, vegetable starches were used to give the garments body and a crisp edge while they were still slightly damp.

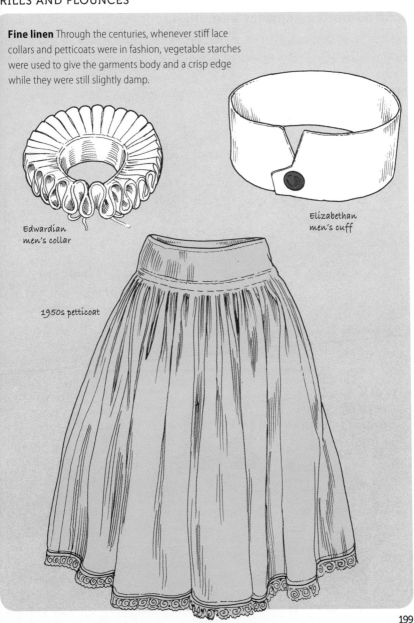

Edwardian
men's collar

Elizabethan
men's cuff

1950s petticoat

WASHING DELICATES

Lingerie and swimwear Separate fragile or expensive garments, such as lacey bras and silk slips, from the rest of the wash so you can give them some special attention.

LINGERIE

Delicates cycle Use a special bra or lingerie bag to protect delicates in the wash. For special items, such as silk, hand wash in warm or cool water with a little shampoo. Roll in a towel before drying.

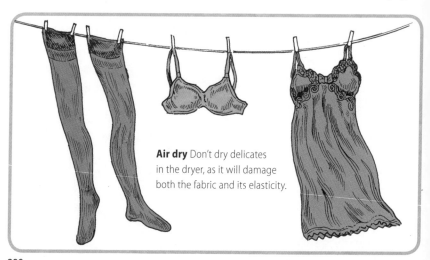

Air dry Don't dry delicates in the dryer, as it will damage both the fabric and its elasticity.

WIMSUITS

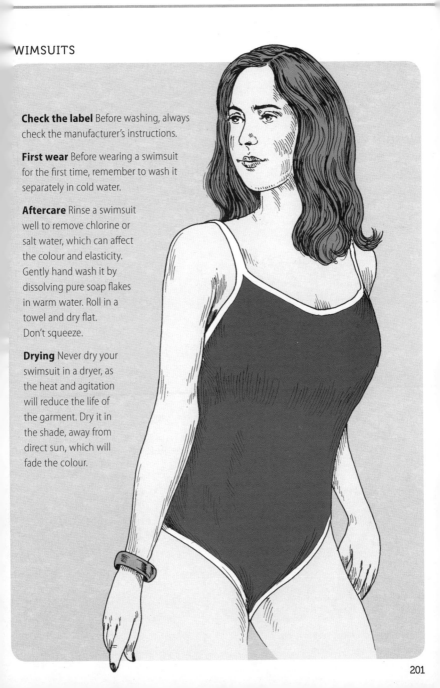

Check the label Before washing, always check the manufacturer's instructions.

First wear Before wearing a swimsuit for the first time, remember to wash it separately in cold water.

Aftercare Rinse a swimsuit well to remove chlorine or salt water, which can affect the colour and elasticity. Gently hand wash it by dissolving pure soap flakes in warm water. Roll in a towel and dry flat. Don't squeeze.

Drying Never dry your swimsuit in a dryer, as the heat and agitation will reduce the life of the garment. Dry it in the shade, away from direct sun, which will fade the colour.

CARING FOR WOOLLENS

Gentle care Keeping woollen jumpers and cardigans, scarves and hats at their best requires more than just careful washing – when a favourite item loses shape or becomes covered in pills, it needs some extra attention.

WASHING A WOOLLEN JUMPER

1 Dissolve pure soap flakes in warm water – about ¼ cup flakes to 2 litres water.

2 Gently squeeze, then rinse the garment a few times in clean water.

3 Use a salad spinner to remove any excess moisture from the garment.

4 Alternatively, squeeze out excess moisture by rolling the garment in a dry towel.

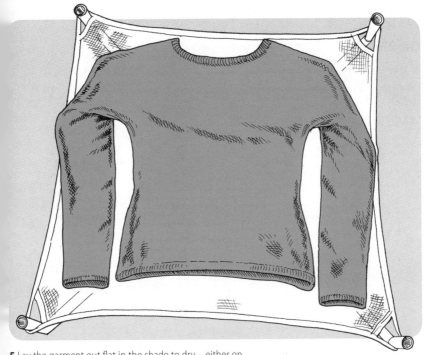

5 Lay the garment out flat in the shade to dry – either on a dry towel or a special mesh rack.

3 WAYS TO DEPILL A WOOLLEN GARMENT

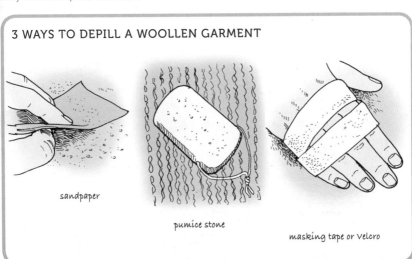

sandpaper

pumice stone

masking tape or Velcro

RESTORING AN OUT-OF-SHAPE CUFF

1 Pour hot, not boiling, water into a bowl.

2 Dampen the cuff only. Don't saturate it.

3 Reshape the cuff, and dry it with a hair dryer.

REBLOCKING A WOOLLEN GARMENT

Pin down the shape Before washing, pull the garment into shape, then measure it. After washing, lay it flat on a board covered with a dry towel, and stretch it to its original dimensions, pinning as you go. Allow it to dry.

OLDING A JUMPER

1 Fold the sleeves into the centre.

2 Fold one side in line with the shoulder.

3 Do the same with the other side.

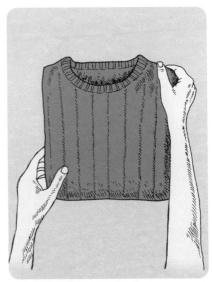

4 Fold in half or thirds, and turn over.

DRYING OUTSIDE

Pegged out Whether you have a couple of lines strung across a small balcony or a revolving family-sized clothesline in a big backyard, the way you hang the washing will help minimise the amount of drying time.

ON THE LINE

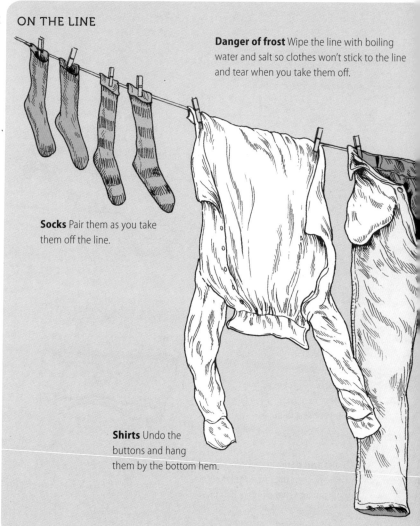

Danger of frost Wipe the line with boiling water and salt so clothes won't stick to the line and tear when you take them off.

Socks Pair them as you take them off the line.

Shirts Undo the buttons and hang them by the bottom hem.

T-shirts and jeans If you smooth them as you take them off the line and fold them into the basket, they may not need ironing.

Knitted top To avoid marking the fabric with pegs, insert an old pair of tights through the sleeves.

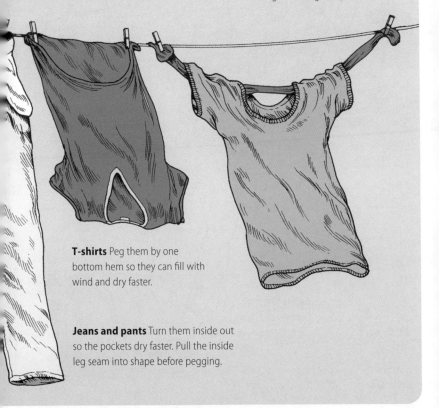

T-shirts Peg them by one bottom hem so they can fill with wind and dry faster.

Jeans and pants Turn them inside out so the pockets dry faster. Pull the inside leg seam into shape before pegging.

DRYING INSIDE

Dryers and clothes airers If you live in an apartment, especially if it's in a cold climate, you'll need to be able to dry clothes inside without making your home look like a commercial laundry.

THE EFFICIENT CLOTHES DRYER

DRYING DELICATES

Drip-dry Hand-washed garments will dry faster on an inflated plastic hanger.

DIY mini line Screw small eye bolts into a wooden hanger, then run twine from one end to the other. Use wooden pegs to hold items.

TYPES OF CLOTHES AIRERS

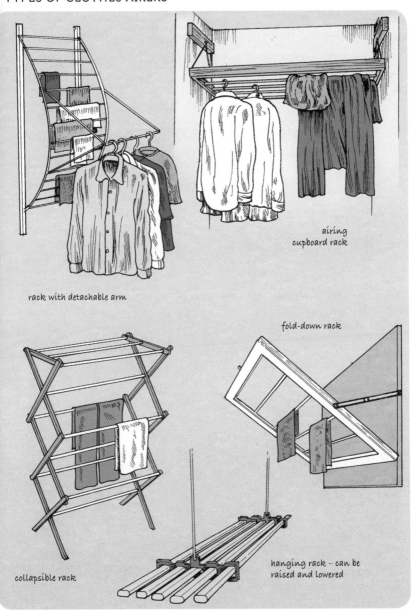

rack with detachable arm

airing
cupboard rack

fold-down rack

collapsible rack

hanging rack – can be
raised and lowered

IRONING

Clothes pressing If you're time-poor or just hate ironing, you might pay someone else to do it for you, or even buy permanent-press garments, but for some people ironing clothes dried in the sun is a relaxing pastime.

IRONING TIPS

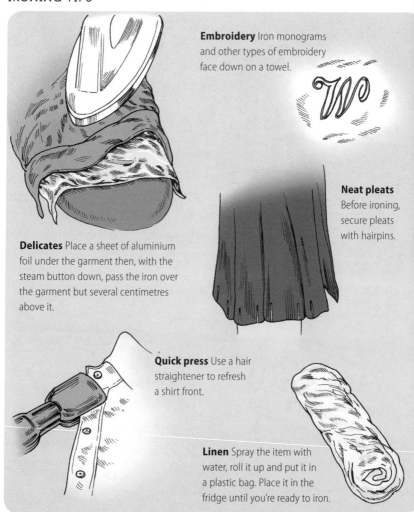

Embroidery Iron monograms and other types of embroidery face down on a towel.

Neat pleats Before ironing, secure pleats with hairpins.

Delicates Place a sheet of aluminium foil under the garment then, with the steam button down, pass the iron over the garment but several centimetres above it.

Quick press Use a hair straightener to refresh a shirt front.

Linen Spray the item with water, roll it up and put it in a plastic bag. Place it in the fridge until you're ready to iron.

IRONING A SHIRT

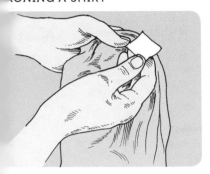

1 Read the care label so you can choose the right heat setting.

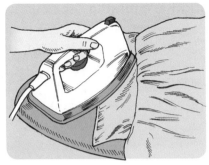

2 Iron the collar on both sides.

3 Iron both sides of the cuffs.

4 Iron both sleeves, on both sides.

5 Iron the shoulders and back.

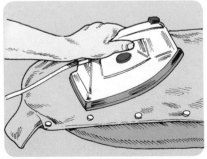

6 Iron both fronts, and hang up.

OLD IRONING TOOLS

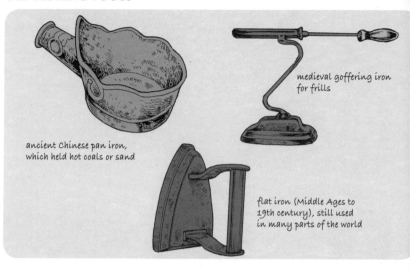

ancient Chinese pan iron, which held hot coals or sand

medieval goffering iron for frills

flat iron (Middle Ages to 19th century), still used in many parts of the world

CLEANING AN IRON

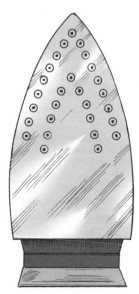

General Clean with a cloth soaked in strong cold tea, then wipe clean.

Brown stains Rub the stains with a cut lemon or scrunched up wax paper.

Melted synthetics Warm the iron and scrape away any solids with a wooden spatula. To remove smaller solids, use a cotton wool bud dipped in nail polish remover.

Rust Scrub the stain with a mix of salt and beeswax.

Melted plastic Sprinkle salt over some aluminium foil and iron it.

Dirty plate Rub it with a paste of bicarb and water.

Clean reservoir Pour in ¼ cup white vinegar and set the iron to the hottest setting. Steam the iron until the reservoir is empty.

PACE-SAVING BOARDS

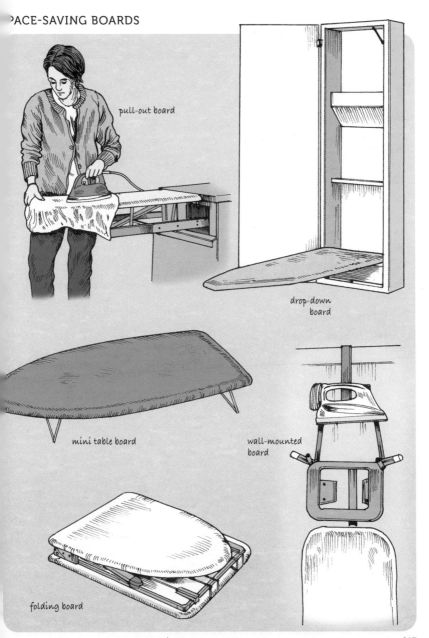

pull-out board

drop-down board

mini table board

wall-mounted board

folding board

Dry-cleaning at home

Non-toxic methods Avoid hazardous dry-cleaning solvents such as 'perc', a known carcinogen, and save money by using fuller's earth, bran, cornflour and salt to clean wool, leather and fur garments.

REVITALISING A WOOL SUIT

Steam clean Brush off any lint and hair, and hang it up to air in a steamy bathroom

THE HOT BRAN AND FLOUR METHOD

1 To clean a wool item, mix together equal quantities of bran and flour, and heat it in the oven.

2 Once it is hot, but not burning, spread it all over the garment.

3 Roll the garment in a towel and leave it for a few days, then shake out the bran and brush it clean.

ARING FOR FUR AND LEATHER

Fur coat Heat some bran in the oven until it is hot but not burning, then gently rub it into the fur. Leave it for an hour or two, then remove it with a soft brush. Hang to air.

Leather jacket Rub a paste made from pipeclay and a little water from the bottom to the top. When the paste is dry, shake the jacket until all the clay has fallen off.

WAYS TO CLEAN A WOOL SKIRT

1 Salt Lay the skirt flat and sprinkle over an even layer of salt. Use a linen pad to rub the salt from the waist to the hem. Hang it up and brush thoroughly.

2 Fuller's earth Use this with water to make a paste that will remove grease and oil. Spread the paste on the garment, and when it is dry, brush it off with a stiff brush.

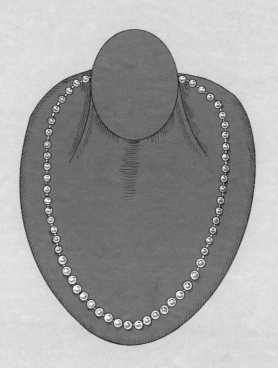

PERSONAL BELONGINGS

These practical items may hold some of your possessions, protect you from the elements or help express your personal style. If you can, invest in quality materials and workmanship.

SHOES

Stepping out Polish leather shoes regularly, and attend to water damage and scratches as soon as you can. And try to spread the wear – your shoes will last longer if they're allowed to 'rest'.

CLEANING TIPS

Deodoriser Add a few drops of antibacterial lavender essential oil to bicarb soda, pack the mix into an old sock and shove it into smelly trainers. Leave overnight.

Patent leather Use vegetable oil to clean and polish patent leather shoes.

Suede Remove small stains with an emery board.

CUSTOMISING YOUR SHOES

Shoe clips Use them to update, revitalise and dress up your shoes. Buy them ready-made or use a pair of blank clips to make your own – perfect for dressing up a pair of evening shoes.

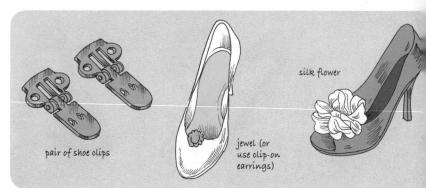

pair of shoe clips

jewel (or use clip-on earrings)

silk flower

‍HOE CARE

Travel protection
Next time you pack
a suitcase, slip dress
shoes into old socks.

Wet shoes Stuff
them with scrunched
up newspaper.

Loose laces To stop laces unravelling,
dab lip balm where you tie them.

Boot supports
Use empty wine
bottles to maintain
the shape of boots.

satin bow

button

feather

Bags, hats and gloves

Accessories The combination of the need for sun protection and the increased popularity of racing carnivals have led to the revival of hats, but bags and gloves are never out of fashion.

GLOVES

Work out your glove size Wrap a tape measure around your fist (excluding your thumb), then measure the length of your longest finger. Take the higher measurement and convert it to inches – for example, if it's 18 cm, or 7 in, that's a size 7 glove. For the best fit, go up half a size.

Cleaning gloves Turn them inside out, then clean them as you would other garments made from the same material. To dry, insert the handle of a wooden spoon into one of the fingers and stand it up in a jar.

BAG TIPS

* **Old leather** To revitalise an old bag, clean it with a solution of washing soda and warm water. Rinse with lukewarm water, air-dry, then rub in some wax polish.
* **Sticky zip** Ease it by rubbing candle wax along the teeth.
* **Plain backpacks and cloth purses** Wash these separately in cold water on the delicates cycle, then air-dry. (Multicoloured backpacks may bleed.)
* **Misshapen handbag** Stuff it with tissue or newspaper, or just use it more often.

AT CARE

Beret To reshape a beret, or to dry one, insert a plate of an appropriate size.

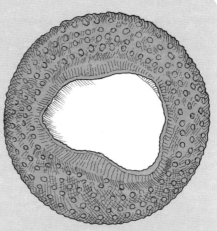

Straw hat To stiffen straw, brush egg white on the wrong side and allow it to dry.

Valuable hat Wrap it in acid-free tissue paper and store it in a hat box.

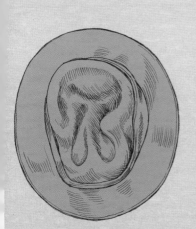

Crushed hat Stuff it with some scrunched up tissue paper.

Scarves and Ties

Neckwear The scarf is not only a versatile accessory but can also have religious significance in many cultures, while the necktie is a descendant of the cravat, first worn by Croatian mercenaries in the 17th century.

COMPACT STORAGE

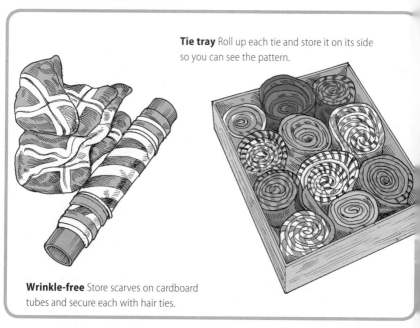

Tie tray Roll up each tie and store it on its side so you can see the pattern.

Wrinkle-free Store scarves on cardboard tubes and secure each with hair ties.

TYING A WINDSOR KNOT

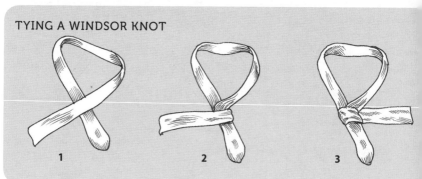

1

2

3

OW TO TIE A CHELSEA KNOT

Fold the scarf in half.

2 Put it around your neck.

3 Pull the ends through the loop.

4 Tighten the loop.

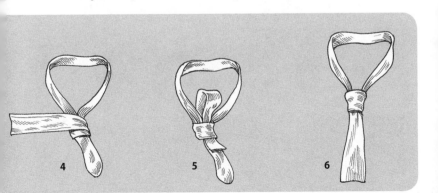

JEWELLERY

Personal adornment A jewellery collection is highly personal, and often features items of sentimental value. Organise yours so it's easier to choose what to wear, and keep it clean and in good condition.

CARE AND CLEANING TIPS

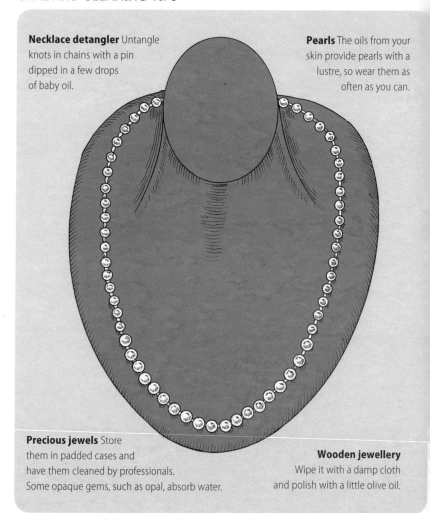

Necklace detangler Untangle knots in chains with a pin dipped in a few drops of baby oil.

Pearls The oils from your skin provide pearls with a lustre, so wear them as often as you can.

Precious jewels Store them in padded cases and have them cleaned by professionals. Some opaque gems, such as opal, absorb water.

Wooden jewellery Wipe it with a damp cloth and polish with a little olive oil.

STORAGE AND DISPLAY

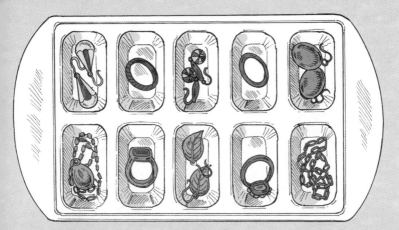

Ice cube tray Here's an inexpensive way to organise earrings and rings.

Tea tray Store jewellery in odd cups and saucers on a tray, or in a drawer. Hang earrings around the cup rims.

Packing

Keep it light A helpful rule of thumb is to pack everything you *think* you
need, then halve it. But however much you take with you, here are some tip[s]
for keeping your clothes and accessories in good condition en route.

STEAMER TRUNKS

Mini wardrobe In the grand days of sea travel, a trunk provided hanging space as well as
drawers for undergarments and accessories. Some types even had secret compartments.

PACKING A SUITCASE

For the first layer, roll up crease-resistant items such as T-shirts and jeans.

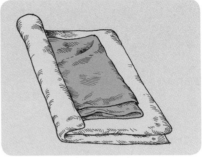

2 Roll up delicate items, such as silk shirts and lingerie, inside other garments.

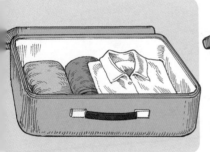

3 Place folded items, such as shirts and jumpers, in the next layer.

4 Lay tailored garments, such as pants and jackets, flat and fold them to fit.

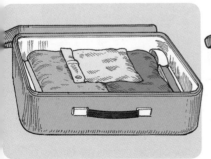

5 Push smaller items, such as books and belts, around the sides of the case.

6 Fill shoes with small items or socks, which will help keep their shape.

HOME DÉCOR

The finishing touches help make your home a warm and inviting one. Create your own style with colour, fresh flowers, candles, pictures, photographs and seasonal decorations.

Repairing plasterboard

Painting prep Before you paint a room, check the walls and ceiling for any holes or cracks that need to be repaired. If you don't clean and prepare the paint surface properly, the paint will eventually crack and flake off.

PATCHING A SMALL HOLE

  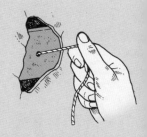

1 Cut a piece of plasterboard that is slightly larger than the hole in one direction so you can angle it into the hole.

2 Drill a small hole in the board, and thread a piece of string through it. Knot the string around a matchstick on the wrong side. Dab some plaster filler around the edges of the back of the hole.

3 Insert the piece in the hole, and pull the string taut while the plaster 'glue' sets. Push the string through to the other side, then start building up the filler bit by bit.

FILLING A SMALL CRACK IN PLASTER

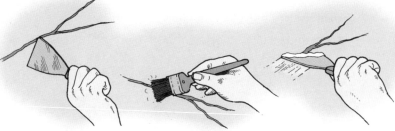

1 Use a paint scraper to open up the cracks, which should be no more than 2 mm wide.

2 Brush away any dust and debris with a paintbrush.

3 Fill the crack with plaster-based filler, and sand smooth.

ATCHING A LARGE HOLE

Remove the damaged part, and use a stanley nife to cut around the hole, making a clean ircular or rectangular hole.

2 Hold a small piece of wood against the back of the wall, and fix it with a plasterboard screw on either side.

3 Cut a piece of plasterboard scrap to fit the hole, and push it into place.

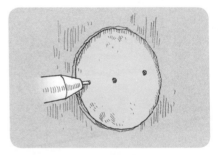

4 Fix the piece of scrap to the wood backing with 2–3 plasterboard screws, which should finish just below the surface of the wall.

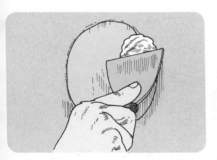

5 Apply plaster-based filler gradually, in layers. The last layer of filler should be slightly proud of the wall surface.

6 Sand smooth, then prime and paint.

Decorating

Basic kit Often the amateur decorator, eager to transform a room in a weekend, can't wait to start slapping paint on the walls, but the whole process will be much more efficient if you assemble the right tools first.

TOOLS FOR THE JOB

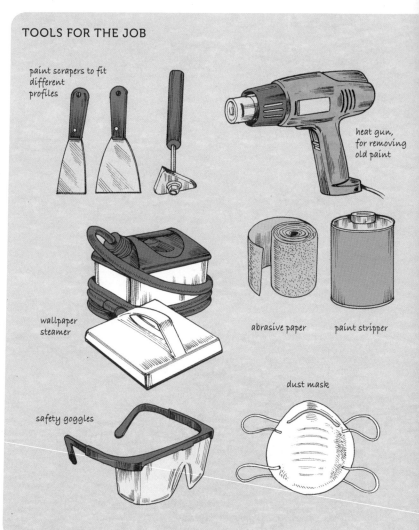

paint scrapers to fit different profiles

heat gun, for removing old paint

wallpaper steamer

abrasive paper

paint stripper

dust mask

safety goggles

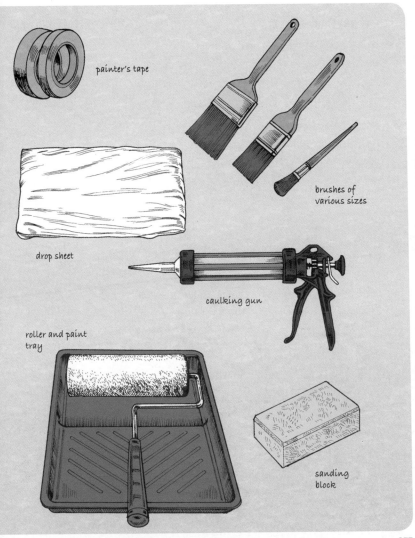

painter's tape

brushes of
various sizes

drop sheet

caulking gun

roller and paint
tray

sanding
block

PAINTING A ROOM

A new look Refreshing a room with paint is one of the cheapest ways to redecorate. For a professional finish, approach the job in a methodical way, working from the ceiling down and cutting in properly as you go.

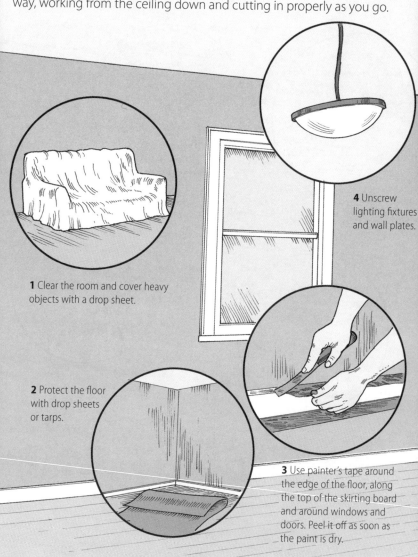

1 Clear the room and cover heavy objects with a drop sheet.

2 Protect the floor with drop sheets or tarps.

3 Use painter's tape around the edge of the floor, along the top of the skirting board and around windows and doors. Peel it off as soon as the paint is dry.

4 Unscrew lighting fixtures and wall plates.

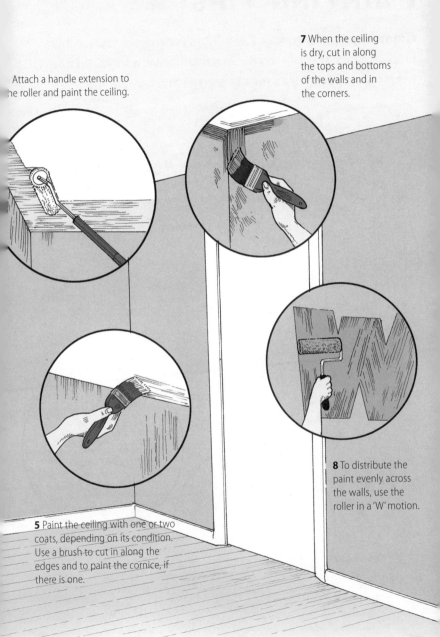

Attach a handle extension to he roller and paint the ceiling.

7 When the ceiling is dry, cut in along the tops and bottoms of the walls and in the corners.

8 To distribute the paint evenly across the walls, use the roller in a 'W' motion.

5 Paint the ceiling with one or two coats, depending on its condition. Use a brush to cut in along the edges and to paint the cornice, if there is one.

Painting tips

Cleaning up Buy good quality brushes and rollers and clean them properly after each use – you don't want your paintwork ruined by stiff bristles or stray brush hairs stuck in dried paint.

Clean rim Place a thick rubber band around the tin, as shown. Alternatively, before pouring paint from the tin, cover part of the rim with masking tape. When you've finished, peel off the tape so there won't be any messy residue making it difficult to close the lid.

Take a break Drill a hole through the brush handle, then insert a stick through the hole and use it to rest the brush in a jar of water or solvent between painting sessions.

Condition the brush Remove any loose hairs from a new brush by brushing it across some abrasive paper a few times.

Catch drips Cut a slit in a plastic lid so it fits snugly around the paintbrush handle.

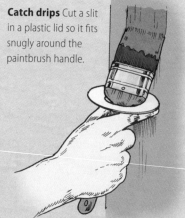

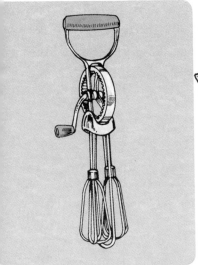

Paint mixer Use an old egg beater rather than a stick to mix a tin of paint.

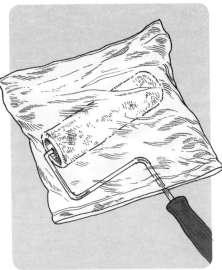

Clean storage Store a paint roller or paintbrush in a plastic bag or plastic wrap.

Colour swatch Dab a little of the paint colour on the lid of the tin – after a year or so, it will mean a lot more to you than the name.

Skinless paint Store the tin of paint upside down on a sheet of plastic to prevent a skin forming. Make sure the lid is secure first.

MILK PAINT

Non-toxic paint Although it has a shelf life of only a few days, milk pain
is completely natural. It has a soft effect with a chalky finish that can be used
to mimic the look of old furniture. Buy a milk-paint kit or make your own.

MAKING MILK PAINT

1 Combine the juice of
1 lemon with 1 litre skim milk
in a large bowl. Leave overnight at room temperature.

2 Strain the curdled mixture
through a sieve lined with
muslin. Discard the curds.

3 Add up to 4 tablespoons dry colour pigment or
experiment with artist's acrylic paint to achieve the
colour you want. Add a small amount each time.

CUSTOMISING RAW FURNITURE

Shabby chic Transform a piece of raw furniture with milk paint, timber moulding and new knobs.

1 Remove the original knobs and any other hardware, then sand and clean with a damp cloth. Attach timber beading or mouldings of your choice.

2 Mix the milk paint (see opposite) and apply lightly with a brush. Allow to dry for 24 hours before lightly sanding and applying a second coat.

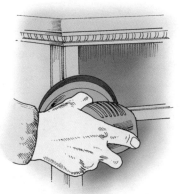

3 Sand lightly or, to achieve a distressed look, go over some areas again.

4 Apply a finish, such as polyurethane. Fix new knobs to the drawers.

SPACE-SAVING IDEAS

Clever storage Apartment living can make choosing and arranging furniture a challenge. Consider pieces that have a dual function, or try to utilise dead space, such as empty cupboards or under the stairs.

UNDER THE STAIRS

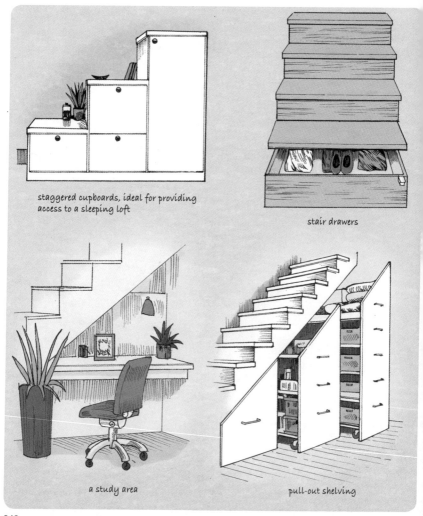

staggered cupboards, ideal for providing access to a sleeping loft

stair drawers

a study area

pull-out shelving

EHIND CLOSED DOORS

ome office Turn a built-in wardrobe into a home office or study
ace – just close the doors when it's not in use. In a small house or
artment a cupboard is also perfect for hiding a washer and dryer.

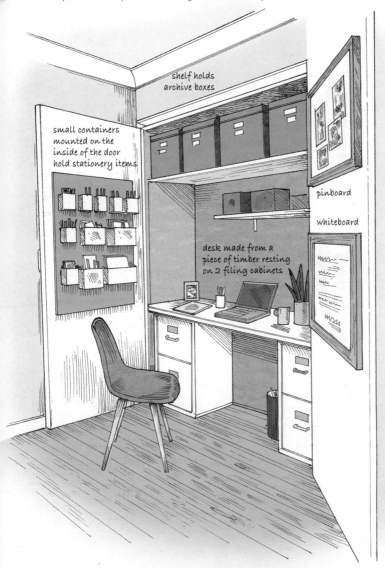

shelf holds
archive boxes

small containers
mounted on the
inside of the door
hold stationery items

pinboard

whiteboard

desk made from a
piece of timber resting
on 2 filing cabinets

EFFICIENT STORAGE

Investment Furniture that performs a dual function can be expensive, but it can also double the potential of the available floor space.

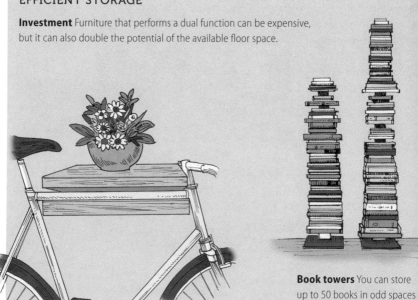

Book towers You can store up to 50 books in odd spaces where a bookcase wouldn't fit

Versatile bike rack A simple notch in a wall-mounted table becomes a bike rack.

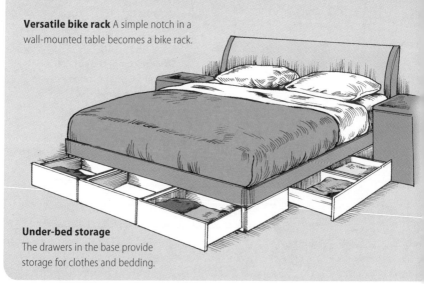

Under-bed storage
The drawers in the base provide storage for clothes and bedding.

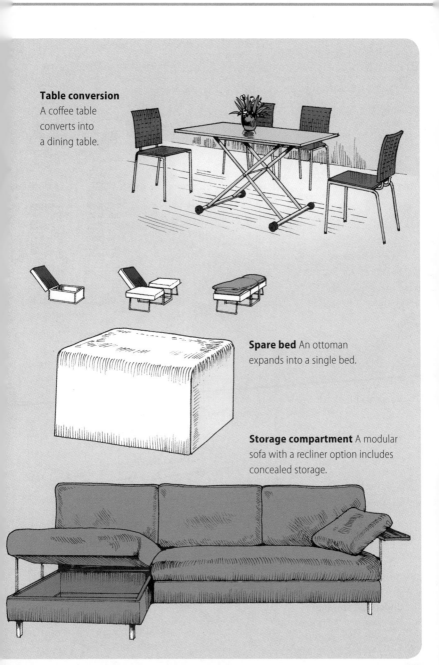

Table conversion
A coffee table
converts into
a dining table.

Spare bed An ottoman
expands into a single bed.

Storage compartment A modular
sofa with a recliner option includes
concealed storage.

THE ILLUSION OF SPACE

Breathing room A small room need not feel like a tiny box. Keep it clean and uncluttered, and consider utilising these useful interior design tips for making it seem larger.

GENERAL TIPS

* Paint the walls in pale colours, and choose a light-coloured floor covering or rug.
* Use a mirror opposite the window to reflect light and, if possible, provide a view.
* Go for simple window treatments, such as a venetian or Roman blind.
* Make a low ceiling seem higher with wall shelving high on the wall, or with a tall cupboard.
* Minimise the amount of furniture in the room – too many small pieces make any space look cluttered and untidy.
* Choose furniture that has more than one purpose – for example, for a combined study/spare room, choose a divan bed with storage drawers in the base.

THE WET PORCH

A transition space The utility room or wet porch, which may be part of a laundry, is the link between outside and your home's interior. Keep it organised with lockers, coathooks and different types of shelving.

LOCKERS

Personal organiser Assign a locker to each member of the household, and expect everyone to keep their area neat and tidy.

top shelves can hold h[...] and books to be return[...] to the library

coathooks, used for drying and storing jackets and bags

wire bins for drying wet shoes

easy-care, non-slip floor

bench allows people to sit while they take off their wet shoes

SEFUL ADDITIONS

A place for everything Keeping the wet porch organised will encourage children to put their things away when they come in, rather than strew them all over the house.

Sports rack Use this to store umbrellas, bats, balls and other sporting equipment.

Drying cabinet You can buy cabinets that dry wet clothes and snow gear by heat, or the ambient type that simply circulates air.

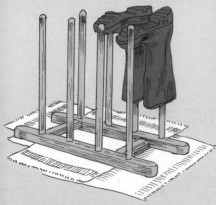

Boot rack Place it on top of old towels, which can catch the drips.

MESSAGE BOARDS

Household organiser Sometimes all those bits of paperwork – bills to be paid, postcards, appointment cards and school notices – can seem overwhelming, but you can make them a well-organised feature.

MAKING YOUR OWN

cover a padded fabric board with a lattice of ribbon

divide a pinboard into sections, one for each person

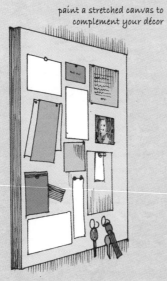

paint a stretched canvas to complement your décor

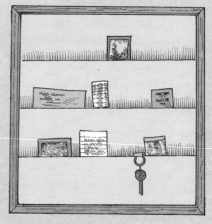

attach simple hessian pockets to a piece of board and then frame it

Recycled frame Create a decorative message board by removing the glass and backing from an old mirror and replacing it with chicken wire or rows of wire fixed to small cup hooks behind the frame. This is a great way to display old postcards.

FLOWERS AND FOLIAGE

From the garden Experiment by using containers other than vases, and try arrangements of lush foliage, such as *Magnolia grandifolia* and *Viburnum* species, twigs and seed pods, which have a striking sculptural effect.

BASIC FLORIST'S KIT

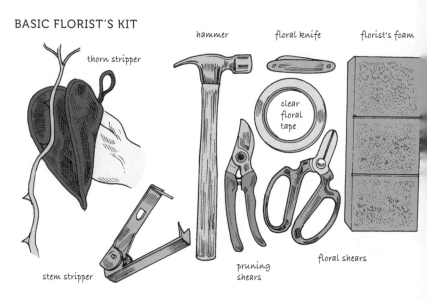

thorn stripper

hammer

floral knife

florist's foam

clear floral tape

stem stripper

pruning shears

floral shears

CUTTING FLOWERS

Keep flowers fresh Cut flowers early in the morning and put them in water straight away. Add flower food or sugar to the water, and change the water every few days.

1 Remove foliage from the lower stems so it won't rot in the water.

2 Cut each stem on a 45 degree angle.

3 Cauterise each stem with a candle flame.

PRACTICAL SUPPORT

Alternatives to florist's foam To hold stems in place, put a criss-cross grid of sticky tape across any vessel (left) – it doesn't have to be a vase – or support long stems in decorative marbles (centre), shells or pebbles (right).

THINK OUTSIDE THE SQUARE

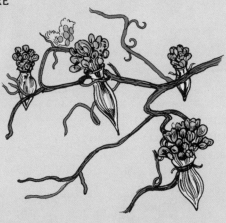

Centrepieces For an unusual table centrepiece, pot up several small succulents in little pots (left), grow some wheat grass in a square box (above left), or tie miniature tear-drop glass shades to spring branches and fill them with buds and little flowers (above).

FLORAL TEA PARTY

Pretty china Create a theme by filling teapots, cups and eggcups with dainty flowers.

SEED PODS AND HEADS

Architectural effect Fresh or dried seed pods and heads add a wonderful sculptural element to arrangements. Use them instead of flowers for an unusual display.

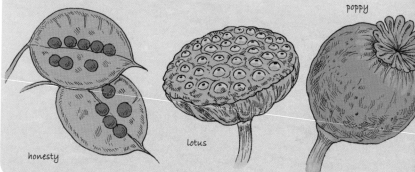

poppy

honesty

lotus

LEAN LINES

Lineal arrangement Team flowers with a sculptural form, such as these calla lilies (*Zantedeschia aethiopica*), with uncluttered, straplike foliage.

GENERAL TIPS

* **Balance** – Keep the shape symmetrical, like the sphere shape at left, and balance the colours and types of flowers in a mixed arrangement. Use odd numbers of flowers – 3, 5, 7 etc – to help keep the whole arrangement balanced.
* **Harmony and unity** – Match the style of the arrangement to the container, and keep colour blends simple and complementary – for example, blue and yellow, and white and green are stunning together.
* **Scale and proportion** – Don't put a small posy in a large vase. Each arrangement should be in proportion to its container.

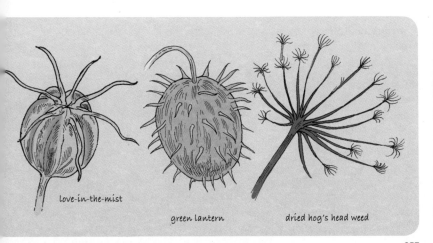

love-in-the-mist

green lantern

dried hog's head weed

CANDLES

Circle of light Soft, shimmering light, often with a subtle fragrance, help
create a calming, intimate mood for relaxation, meditation and of course
entertaining, and it's fun and easy to make your own.

MAKING TEACUP CANDLES

Tools and materials For
this project you'll need a
candle-making kit, including
wax, wicks and metal tabs,
plus teacups, wooden
skewers and scissors.

1 Cut a length of wick to suit the depth of the
cup, plus a little extra for securing it to the skewer.
2 Tie one end of the wick to the skewer and secure
the other to the metal tab.
3 Place the skewer across the top of the cup
(as shown above).

4 Follow the manufacturer's directions
for melting the wax, and pour in enough
melted wax to fill the cup.
5 Pull the skewer out of the knot and trim
the wick. This is a great way to use odd
teacups, with or without the saucer.

AKING A CANDLE WITH A BALLOON

Fill the balloon with water and tie it off. Attach tring or wire securely to the end. Melt the wax ccording to the manufacturer's directions, and ool it to 65°C.

2 Holding the balloon by the string, dip it into the wax for a second then slowly remove it. Allow to cool for a minute or so, then dip it again. Keep dipping until you're happy with the amount of wax on the balloon – about 5 mm.

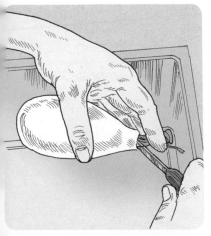

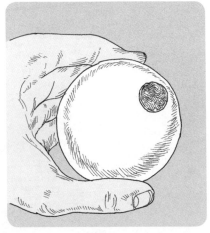

3 When it is cool, use the point of a sharp knife to puncture the ballon. Pour out the water and carefully remove the balloon.

4 Again, use a sharp knife to enlarge the size of the hole so you can place a votive candle inside the fine wax shell.

PARTY LIGHTS

Set the mood Candles not only cast a soft, flattering light but can also create a romantic, magical atmosphere, ideal for parties. For a summer party outdoors, float tea lights and flowers in a birdbath in a sheltered corner of the garden.

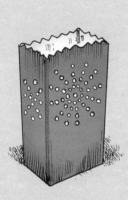

Light the way Guide party guests along the path or up stairs with candles in paper bags (above left), glass jars, vases (above right) or punctured tins (see page 45).

Massed display Use a tiered cake stand to display candles of different heights.

Pedestal lights Place votive candles on a bed of sand within each glass.

AKING HANGING LIGHTS

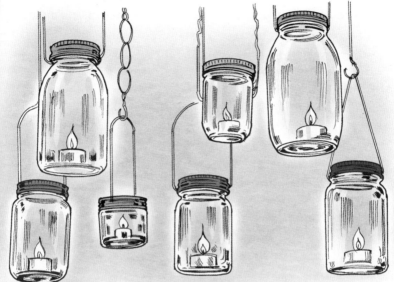

pecial event This is an effective but inexpensive way to make party lights, which look great
anging from a pergola or the branches of a tree. You'll need an odd assortment of jars, tea lights
r candle stumps and 24-gauge wire. Puncture the lids so the candles will have oxygen to burn.

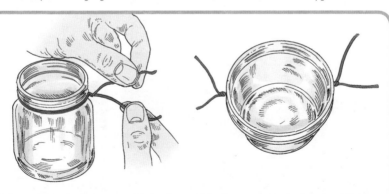

1 Wrap one length of wire around the neck of the jar, and twist the short end around the long end. The length of wire depends on where you're hanging the jar.

2 Do the same with another piece of wire the same length. Use pliers to trim the short ends. Twist the long ends together to form the handle.

ART AND PHOTOGRAPHS

Conserve and display Create a home gallery by following these easy tips on hanging pictures, then consider how you could make the most of your collection of children's art and digital photographs.

HANGING CONFIGURATIONS

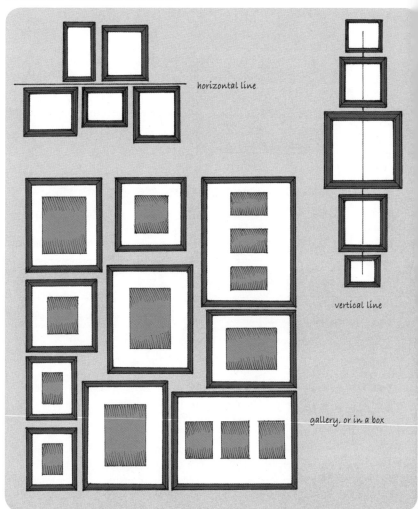

horizontal line

vertical line

gallery, or in a box

ANGING PICTURES THE EASY WAY

olproof method Use this paper template technique to both perfect your arrangement
d place the picture hooks in precisely the right place.

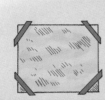

1 Use a level to check all the templates are on straight.

2 Use painter's tape, which won't mark the wall, to attach each template.

point where wire is tautest

3 Transpose these vertical and horizontal measurements from the back of each picture to its corresponding template.

4 Fix picture hooks while the templates are in place, then gently remove the paper.

GENERAL TIPS

* Unite a disparate group of pictures by using the same framing style.
* Play around with the arrangement on the floor until you're happy, or attach paper templates to the wall. Devise some way to describe each template so you know which picture is which.
* To work out where the hook should go, measure and mark the paper template as shown above.

CHILDREN'S ART

The creative impulse If your fridge door is too small to showcase your children's efforts, here are some other ways to display and preserve them.

Cushion Scan a favourite picture and use the digital print to make soft furnishings.

Art cabinet and frame Use one to store and display up to 50 pieces.

Book Make a collection that will last a lifetime. Search for online companies that offer this service.

Clipboard Use one or several so you can change the display regularly.

Curtain rail Turn a wall into an art gallery with a curtain rail and clips. On a blank wall, you could install several rows.

DIGITAL PHOTOGRAPHS

Feature canvas Have a favourite portrait or photo printed onto a stretched canvas.

Computer Store photos on DVDs, make slide shows, and share photos with friends and family on photo-sharing websites.

Album Print them out and collect them in a traditional album, or make a book (see opposite).

Software Experiment with different effects in your picture-processing software and manipulate images.

BEFORE YOU GO AWAY

Preparing to leave It's important to prepare the house as well as cance mail and newspaper deliveries so they don't mount up on your doorstep an make it obvious to thieves that you're away.

CHECKLIST

1 Ask the post office to hold your mail, or redirect it to another address.

2 Cancel newspaper deliveries, and ask a neighbour to collect junk mail.

3 Ask a neighbour to keep an eye on your home, and give them your contact details.

4 Set up timers on a selection of lights but make sure you vary the rooms and times.

Check all the taps are turned off properly, and x any leaks.

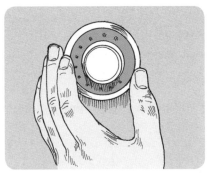

6 Reduce the thermostat on the hot water heater, or turn it off.

7 Empty the fridge of perishables – give them away rather than throw them out.

8 Check that all windows and exterior doors are locked and secure.

9 Turn off all appliances at the power point or they will still use power and cost you money.

10 Check your insurance policies – building, contents and car – are all up to date.

CHRISTMAS DECORATIONS

Festive cheer Handmade decorations and special treats can enhance the pleasure of Christmas. Welcome guests with a wreath at the front door, bake a gingerbread house and delight the children with an advent calendar.

BUILDING A GINGERBREAD HOUSE

Make a template Use cardboard to make a plan of the major pieces first – the walls and roof – then use a favourite recipe for gingerbread. Roll out the dough and cut out the pieces according to your plan. Assemble the pieces with icing 'glue' (see opposite).

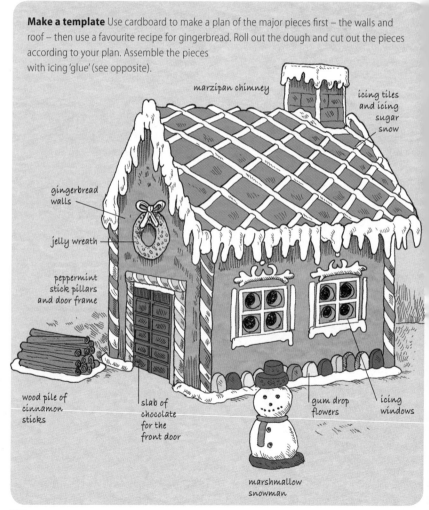

marzipan chimney

icing tiles and icing sugar snow

gingerbread walls

jelly wreath

peppermint stick pillars and door frame

wood pile of cinnamon sticks

slab of chocolate for the front door

gum drop flowers

icing windows

marshmallow snowman

AKING ICING 'GLUE'

1 In a bowl, separate 3 eggs and set aside all the yolks.

2 Combine 450 g icing sugar and 1 teaspoon cream of tartar with the egg whites.

3 Beat until the mixture is stiff.

4 If it starts to harden, add a little water.

ADVENT CALENDARS

Christmas treats Children love the thrill of opening a window, or pulling out a little box, and discovering a small favour on each of the 25 days of Christmas. Rather than purchase a commercial calendar, consider making your own. These ideas will help get you started.

Matchboxes Cover each box with decorative paper, and thread a numbered bead onto a piece of string. Secure it with a knot on the inside of the drawer. Place a favour in the drawer, close it and hang it from the tree.

Mini Christmas stockings Use 25 baby or children's socks in different colours and patterns. Attach to a ribbon with mini pegs.

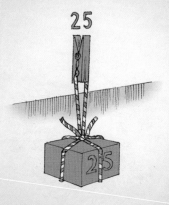

Little parcels Wrap each favour, label it with a number, and hang it from the Christmas tree.

Pockets Cut out pieces of a sturdy fabric such as felt, embroider each with a number, then sew the little pockets onto a larger backing piece. Put a favour in each pocket.

MAKING A CHRISTMAS WREATH

Seasonal welcome You can make a wreath out of almost anything – from evergreen foliage and fabric to newspaper and strips of plastic bag, but here's how to make a traditional wreath for the front door.

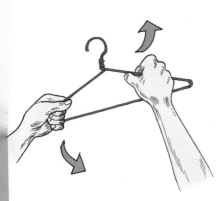

1 Stretch a coathanger into a circle, or use a florist's wreath if you prefer.

2 Layer the foliage and berries so that they point in one direction – either clockwise or anticlockwise.

3 As you go, secure the foliage with some florist's wire.

4 Hang the finished wreath on the front door.

EASTER EGGS

Traditional crafts Supervise the children while they work with paints, crayons, dyes, hot wax and elastic bands to make beautiful hand-decorated eggs, then use them to adorn the table on Easter Sunday.

PAINTING DESIGNS WITH WAX

Wax-resist dyeing Draw designs or write on eggs with wax, before dipping the eggs in dye. You'll need a pinhead stuck in the wrong end of a pencil, a candle and match, some dye (see opposite), and hard-boiled eggs.

1 Dip the pinhead in melted candle wax and draw a design on the egg.

2 When the wax is dry, dip the egg in the dye. Allow the dye to dry.

3 Use tongs to hold the egg over a candle flame and wipe off the wax as it melts.

DECORATING WITH LEAVES AND FLOWERS

1 Use a small paintbrush to paint one side of the leaf with egg white. Stick it on the clean eggshell.

2 Insert the egg in a section of stocking, knotting it at each end. Dip it in the dye for 5 minutes.

3 When you're happy with the colour, remove the stocking, then carefully peel off the leaf and allow the egg to dry on a wire rack.

MAKING NATURAL DYES

* Add 2 tablespoons of each spice, or 3½ cups fruit, to 2 cups water, and boil for 5 minutes. Remove from heat, strain if necessary, and add 1 tablespoon vinegar before soaking the eggs. The longer you leave it, the darker the colour.

* Blue – blueberries
* Yellow – turmeric
* Orange – paprika
* Pink – raspberries

OTHER TECHNIQUES

Elastic band Dye the egg, then wind a rubber band around it, and dye it with another colour.

Masking tape Cut the tape into simple graphic designs and stick them to the egg before dyeing.

 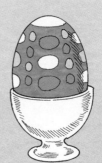

Paint Using a fine brush and artist's acrylic or oil paints, paint a design onto the egg.

OUTDOORS

A well-designed, lovingly maintained garden is a delight. Whether you have a suburban plot or a compact courtyard, there are many ways to make the most of your outdoor space.

Outdoor Entertaining

The outdoor kitchen If you live in a warm climate you can cook and dine outdoors for many months of the year, so it's worth taking some time and effort to plan your entertaining area carefully.

SITING A BARBECUE

The basics When planning and installing a new barbecue, consider lighting and shelter.

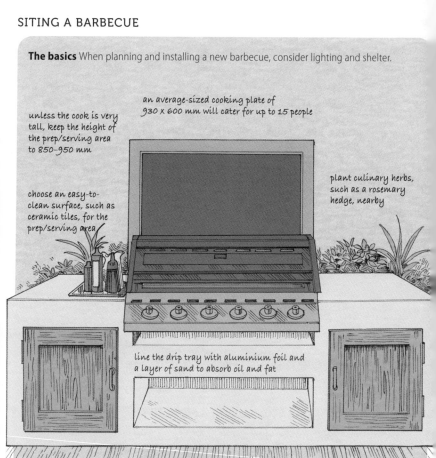

an average-sized cooking plate of 930 x 600 mm will cater for up to 15 people

unless the cook is very tall, keep the height of the prep/serving area to 850–950 mm

plant culinary herbs, such as a rosemary hedge, nearby

choose an easy-to-clean surface, such as ceramic tiles, for the prep/serving area

line the drip tray with aluminium foil and a layer of sand to absorb oil and fat

store fuel – wood or gas bottles – in the cupboard

in front of the barbecue, go for a durable, non-slip surface, such as brick, concrete pavers or timber decking

if you're building your own from bricks, bear in mind that 1 brick course = 75 mm

CLEANING THE BARBECUE

Establish a routine Food-encrusted barbecues attract vermin. At the end of each cooking session, clean the plates and racks so they're ready to use next time. Finish with a light coating of oil, which will help prevent rust.

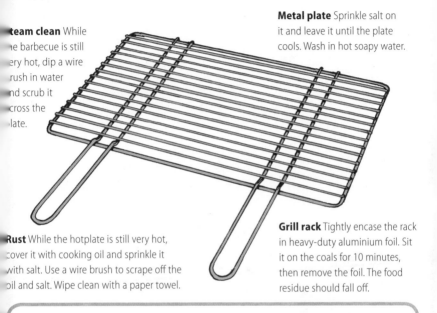

Steam clean While the barbecue is still very hot, dip a wire brush in water and scrub it across the plate.

Metal plate Sprinkle salt on it and leave it until the plate cools. Wash in hot soapy water.

Rust While the hotplate is still very hot, cover it with cooking oil and sprinkle it with salt. Use a wire brush to scrape off the oil and salt. Wipe clean with a paper towel.

Grill rack Tightly encase the rack in heavy-duty aluminium foil. Sit it on the coals for 10 minutes, then remove the foil. The food residue should fall off.

BUILDING A SIMPLE FIRE PIT

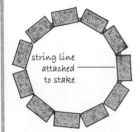

string line attached to stake

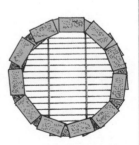

1 Using the size of the grill plate as a guide, mark out the circle of your pit with a string line. Lay the first course of bricks.

2 Lay the second course by overlapping the first. Continue adding courses in the same way.

3 When you're happy with the height, add the grill rack or plate, then secure it with another course of bricks.

CLEANING OUTDOOR FURNITURE

Storage Only store clean, dry furniture so it doesn't develop mould and mildew.

Canvas Treat mildew stains with a paste of bicarb and water. Rinse off after an hour.

Aluminium Scrub off dirt with a solution of warm water and a splash of vinegar.

Timber At the end of winter, scrub with water and allow to dry. Lightly sand the timber, then apply a 4:1 solution of linseed oil thinned with mineral turpentine.

Cane Wash cane with a solution of ¼ cup salt and 1 tablespoon washing soda to 1 litre water. When dry, apply linseed oil. Rinse off. Leave it to dry in the shade, then apply furniture polish.

Wicker Vacuum it then scrub it with soapy water, but try not to saturate the wicker. Keep it covered when it's not in use.

TABLE SPACE

Room to move With any table setting, allow at least 1 m between the edge of the table and the edge of the paving. If you have a small courtyard, consider installing built-in bench seating.

HARD SURFACES

pick and span Keep paved areas clean, as slippery surfaces can cause falls. Sweep them regularly, and attend to any problems as they arise.

Weeds between pavers Pour over some boiling water. The weeds will yellow and die without affecting any other plants.

Grease and oil stains Spread a paste of water and equal parts bicarb soda and fuller's earth on stains. Allow to dry, then brush off any residue.

Mossy pavers Paint on a solution of ¼ cup salt to 5 parts water and 1 part vinegar. When it's dry, sweep away the moss.

MOSQUITO CONTROL

Pet bowls Refresh them daily.

Water features Stock ponds with fish to eat the mosquitoes. Scrub birdbaths weekly.

Carnivorous plants Grow venus fly trap or pitcher plant (above).

Citronella candles Place them around outdoor eating areas.

SMALL TREES FOR COURTYARDS

Added value Maximise the impact of trees by choosing ones with ornamental foliage, flowers or fruit.

Japanese maple *Acer palmatum* grows to 10 m, depending on the cultivar. Some varieties grow well in pots. Cool to subtropical.

Crab apple *Malus floribunda* bears pretty spring blossom and fruit that can be made into jams and jellies. Cool to temperate. To 4 m.

Japanese apricot *Prunus mume* 'Benichidori' flowers in winter on bare stems. Cool to temperate. To 4 m.

FORMAL COURTYARD

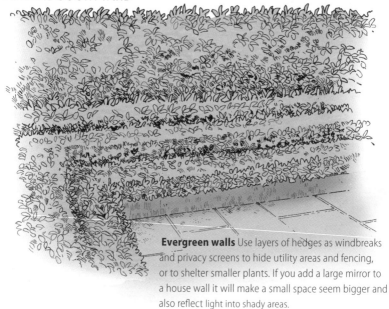

Evergreen walls Use layers of hedges as windbreaks and privacy screens to hide utility areas and fencing, or to shelter smaller plants. If you add a large mirror to a house wall it will make a small space seem bigger and also reflect light into shady areas.

STRONG CLIMBERS FOR PERGOLAS

Winter sun Cover a pergola with a deciduous climber, so you can catch any available sun in the cooler months. Or why not grow a fruiting climber, such as grape?

Rosa filipes **'Kiftsgate'** A white-flowering single rambling rose, it can grow up to 5 m.

Trachelospermum jasminoides In spring this dense evergreen climber is covered in small white flowers.

Campsis **x** *tagliabuana* **'Madame Galen'** A hardy frost-tolerant climber, it bears salmon trumpet flowers in summer.

Wisteria floribunda In spring, pendulous lavender flowers hang from this deciduous vine. Prune it back hard each winter.

Vitis vinifera You may have to net your grapevine in summer to keep the birds away. In subtropical climates with high humidity powdery mildew is a problem.

Actinidia deliciosa The fruit of Chinese gooseberry, a deciduous vine, mature in late summer into autumn. You'll need both a male and female plant.

GARDENING IN POTS

Containers Flourishing plants in well-chosen and carefully positioned pots can add a touch of style to an entrance, help an outdoor dining area fee more intimate and add interest to an otherwise simple courtyard or balcony

GENERAL TIPS

Rootball ratio Always pot plants into containers that are 5 cm larger than the diameter of the rootball.

Mobility If you need to move a large pot around to catch the sun, place it on a plant stand fitted with castors.

Visual interest Stagger the heights of pots. Use pedestals, or turn over a pot and use it to support another one.

Repetition and unity Plant geraniums in terracotta pots, for example, rather than a random selection in odd pots.

Plant labels Flatten old spoons with a hammer and use a metal stamper to etch the labels.

Pot shape Tall tapered pots will restrict the growth of the root system and, after a few years, you'll have to repot.

MAKING HYPERTUFA POTS

DIY stone Hypertufa mimics the look of aged stone over time (tufa is a type of volcanic rock) but is light and cold-hardy (down to −30°C). You'll need a polystyrene box (or similar) for the mould, vegetable oil, 4 parts perlite and 4 parts peat moss to 3 parts cement plus sufficient water to make a mixture that you can mould with your hands.

1 Mix together the ingredients. Spray the mould with some vegetable oil so it will be easier to remove when the hypertufa is dry.

2 Press the hypertufa into the shape of the mould. Push 1–2 pieces of dowel into the base. These will be the drainage holes.

3 Cover the mould with a plastic bag for 48 hours. Remove the bag and dowels, and allow to dry for about 2–3 weeks.

'AGEING' A TERRACOTTA POT

Yogurt Paint on yogurt with a paintbrush, and put the pot in the shade for about a month. By then the pot should have taken on a mellow patina.

Moss Mix together buttermilk and ground up moss, then paint the mixture onto the pot with a foam brush. Put it in the shade until you're happy with the result.

Wood stain Paint it on with a brush or rag. Wipe off any excess to achieve the look you want.

CHILDREN'S PLAY AREAS

Creative play Children love secret places and physical challenges. Provid[e] them with some simple play equipment, such as a sandpit, or use plants an[d] other natural features to create spaces that will stimulate their imagination.

BUILDING A LIVE WILLOW TUNNEL

Hiding place Mark out the walls of the tunnel. Dig a shallow trench about 30 cm wide where you plan to plant the willow rods. For a 3.5 m tunnel, use 15 rods spaced 25 cm apart. The rods should be long enough to be twined together, but still high enough so children can run through the tunnel without bending over.

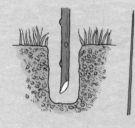  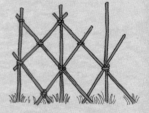

1 Plant the rods 15 cm deep, turning them so they'll grow naturally towards each other to form an arch.

2 Twine the ends of each arch around each other and secure them with cable ties.

3 For extra stability, plant extra rods and train them diagonally across the original structure. Secure the grid with ties.

ATURAL PLAYSCAPES

Simple ideas Stagger stepping stones or logs at different heights (below); grow a weeping tree, such as an elm or mulberry, which is also good for climbing, or runner beans on a wigwam (right); or plant a tall-growing crop such as sunflower or sweetcorn in a circle to create a private space (bottom).

bean wigwam

stepping logs

sunflower circle

WADING POOL

Water play Position a wading pool in the shade and supervise your children at all times. Clean it with a solution of ¼ cup bicarbonate of soda in 4 litres of water.

SANDPIT

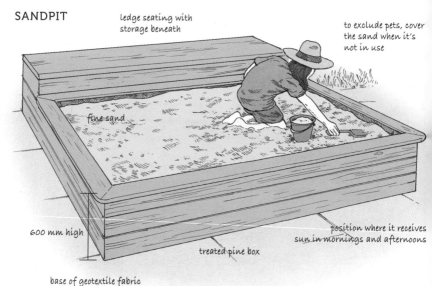

ledge seating with storage beneath

to exclude pets, cover the sand when it's not in use

fine sand

600 mm high

treated pine box

position where it receives sun in mornings and afternoons

base of geotextile fabric

DIY project With the right tools, a sandpit is relatively easy to build. Bear in mind the guidelines above.

ANGING A TYRE SWING

ecycled play equipment If you have a sturdy tree in your garden or on your nature strip, nsider hanging an old tyre as a swing.

First, clean the tyre, then drill drainage holes in what will e the bottom.

2 Thread the rope through some rubber tubing to stop it from fraying.

3 Pass the rope over a sturdy branch about 3–4 m high. Keep the tubing centred over the branch.

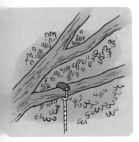

4 Secure the rope over the branch wth a square knot (see the instructions below).

5 Hang the tyre with the holes at the bottom, securing it with another square knot.

6 To cushion any falls, add a thick layer of organic mulch to the ground under the swing.

TYING A SQUARE KNOT

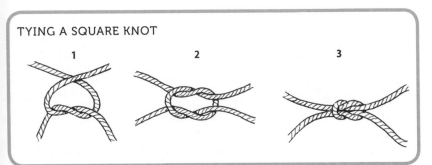

1   2   3

WATER FEATURES

Life force Whether it's still or moving, water adds a peaceful element to any garden, attracting birds and other wildlife and also reflecting the sky, which can make a small courtyard seem bigger.

PORTABLE POND

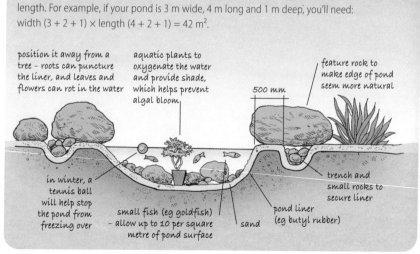

washtub

half wine barrel

stone bowl

Water bowls If your garden is too small for an in-ground pond, consider these ideas. To waterproof your container, apply three coats of waterproofing membrane to a clean, dry surface.

MAKING AN INFORMAL POND

The liner Once you've dug the hole, calculate the amount of pond liner you'll need. Add twice the depth to both the width and length, then add 1 m to both the width and length. For example, if your pond is 3 m wide, 4 m long and 1 m deep, you'll need: width $(3 + 2 + 1) \times$ length $(4 + 2 + 1) = 42$ m².

position it away from a tree – roots can puncture the liner, and leaves and flowers can rot in the water

aquatic plants to oxygenate the water and provide shade, which helps prevent algal bloom

feature rock to make edge of pond seem more natural

500 mm

in winter, a tennis ball will help stop the pond from freezing over

small fish (eg goldfish) – allow up to 10 per square metre of pond surface

sand

pond liner (eg butyl rubber)

trench and small rocks to secure liner

SWIMMING POOLS

An expensive feature Before installing a backyard swimming, plunge or lap pool, consider the site, plantings and safety issues as well as the ongoing cost of maintaining it.

Outdoor shower You can buy kits – even solar-heated ones – that connect to an outdoor tap.

Childproof fence This is mandatory in many areas. Check with your local government authority.

glass safety fence with galvanised or stainless-steel fixings

plants that cope with salt water or chlorine, such as palm trees, succulents and cordylines

non-slip paver that withstands either salt or chlorine, or install timber decking

Screens

Versatile feature Many gardens have an ugly view – a utility area, a boundary fence or even the neighbour's kitchen window – that requires some sort of screen. Grow a hedge, or build a screen yourself.

TRELLIS SCREENS

Decorative patterns You can either attach a wire trellis to a wall, or build a freestanding one between posts. Use it to train climbing plants, or even espaliered fruit trees (see also page 151).

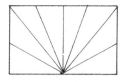 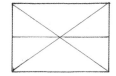 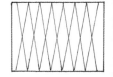

SECURING THE WIRE

1 Use a vine eye in a timber or masonry wall, but for the latter you'll need to plug the wall first.

2 Alternatively, use an eye bolt, which expands within the drilled hole.

3 Use turnbuckles to tighten the wires.

TYING TOGETHER BAMBOO POLES

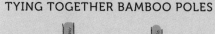

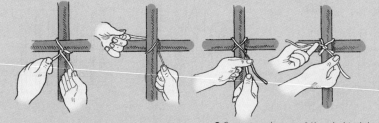

1 Twist the two ends behind the joint.

2 Bring the ends to the front.

3 Cross over the left end.

4 Knot behind the joint, and trim.

AKING A BAMBOO LATTICE SCREEN

Dig post holes, place the osts and level (see page 291).

2 Cement in the holes (again, see page 291).

3 Cut the crosspieces at a 45 degree angle.

Drill into the crosspieces.

5 Screw each crosspiece into the posts at either end.

6 Cut and place the poles, alternating the positions.

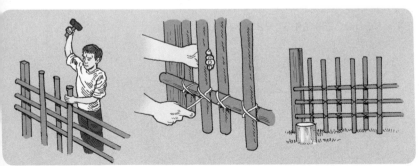

7 Use a mallet to drive the poles into the ground.

8 Tie each juncture (see opposite).

9 Finish the trellis with a coat of preservative.

THE GARDEN SHED

Handy tools Mounting tools on a shadow board or an old piece of garden trellis is a great way to store them. Never leave them out in the weather, or the timber handles will split and the metal parts will rust.

ESSENTIAL GARDEN EQUIPMENT

hand fork

trowel

secateurs

pruning saw

fork

rake

spade

mallet

shears

wire brush

watering can

string

garden gloves

OOL CARE

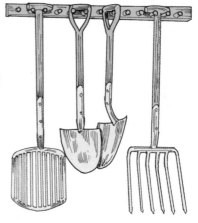

ucket Pour enough egetable oil into a ucket of sand to make a tiff mix. Store hand tools n the bucket – the sand elps wipe off soil residue nd the oil helps prevents hem from rusting.

Spot the tools Paint the handles of tools bright colours – those with brown and green handles are easily lost in the garden.

Pegs and hooks Hang larger tools from pegs, or from hooks on a rail.

SHARPENING TOOLS

Get the edge You must have sharp tools for making clean cuts on plants, especially trees.

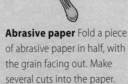

Whet stone Dismantle the secateurs and sharpen each blade in motor oil on the stone at a 20 degree angle.

Abrasive paper Fold a piece of abrasive paper in half, with the grain facing out. Make several cuts into the paper.

Car wax To stop secateurs from sticking, rub some car wax on the hinge.

GARDEN TASKS

Useful techniques Even in a small garden it's handy to know how to deal with a boggy corner or clip a hedge, repair a fence or even lay pavers in a courtyard.

DRAINAGE PROBLEMS

Solutions If an area in your garden is constantly wet and boggy, there are several solutions – you could build a pond (see page 284), plant bog-loving plants, build raised beds, install an agricultural drain or dig a soakaway.

Agricultural drain

1 Dig a trench the width of the spade, and line it with geotextile material with enough extra to wrap over both the pipe and backfill.

2 Lay down a length of agricultural pipe, which may or may not be perforated.

3 Backfill with crushed gravel and lay the fabric over the top. This prevents silt from clogging the drain. Finish with a patch of turf or topsoil.

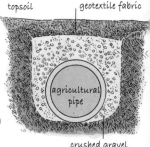

topsoil   geotextile fabric

agricultural pipe

crushed gravel

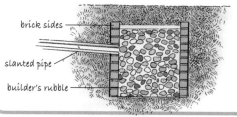

brick sides

slanted pipe

builder's rubble

Soakaway

Direct drainage pipes into a main pipe that empties into a pit filled with builder's rubble. The top 15 cm should be sand and garden soil.

SETTING OUT

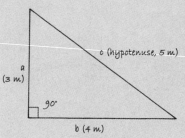

c (hypotenuse, 5 m)

a
(3 m)

90°

b (4 m)

Pythagoras's theorem Use the 3:4:5 rule to help check that corners are square.

1 Using 2 string lines at right angles to each other, measure 4 m down one line and 3 m down the other. The b line is the main line – say, the back wall of a raised garden bed.

2 Measure between these 2 points – if your corner is square, the hypotenuse should be 5 m.

3 If it's out, adjust the position of the a or 3 m line.

GGING POST HOLES

sic skill Post holes are required for many jobs around the garden – for example, installing a
terbox, fencing, pergolas and other garden features. First, set out the position of each post hole
e 'Setting out', opposite).

Use a post hole shovel to dig a hole for
ach post. Make each hole twice the width
f the post and deep enough to take a
hird of the post's length.

2 Embed the post in the bottom of the hole
with some building rubble. Brace the post
upright, as shown. Pour quick-set concrete
into the hole.

3 Use a spirit level to check that the post is
vertical. If necessary, adjust.

4 Add water to the hole, and leave to set.
When dry, remove the braces.

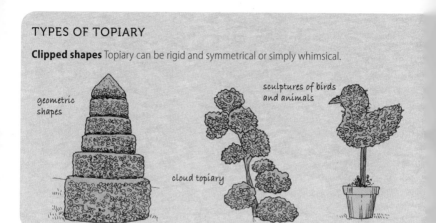

TYPES OF TOPIARY

Clipped shapes Topiary can be rigid and symmetrical or simply whimsical.

geometric shapes

sculptures of birds and animals

cloud topiary

TRIMMING A FORMAL HEDGE

Helpful hints Start from the bottom so the trimmings fall clear of the hedge – if you leave them, they can cause disease. To allow light to reach all the parts, trim the hedge so that it's wider at the base than at the top.

1 Push bamboo canes into the hedge to mark the top edge.

2 Tie a taut string line between the canes.

3 Wearing safety goggles and gloves, use a hedge trimmer in a horizontal sweeping action.

4 Starting at the bottom, which should be wider than the top, trim the sides.

Orchard ladder If you have tall formal hedges, consider investing in one of these.

292

...AVERS

...rick edging Lay out the edge with a string
...ne. Dig a trench about 300 mm wide and
...0 mm deep. Compact the base.
...ay mortar on the base and the
...des of each brick as you go. Fill
...ny gaps with mortar, and sponge
...f any excess.

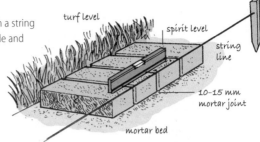

turf level

spirit level

string
line

10–15 mm
mortar joint

mortar bed

...aving styles Before laying a garden path or paved entertaining area, choose a style that will
...uit the style of your garden and the architecture of your house. For example, recycled bricks in
...stretcher bond suit an older style house while stack bond complements sleek modern styles.

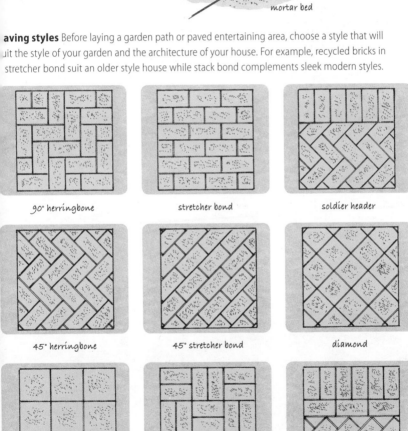

90° herringbone

stretcher bond

soldier header

45° herringbone

45° stretcher bond

diamond

stack bond

basket weave

pencil line inlay

ORGANIC PEST CONTROL

Traditional tips A chemical-free garden is relatively easy to manage, and if you don't use poisonous chemicals to control pests, they can be safely devoured by natural predators such as wasps and birds.

NATURAL SOLUTIONS

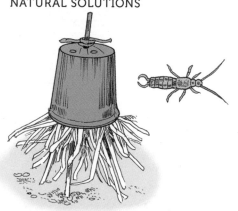

Earwigs These pests like to hide in dark places during the day. Stuff pots with newspaper or straw, turn them upside down and mount them on a stick. Check the pots each day, and drown any earwigs you find.

Rabbits Dig a 30-cm trench around the veggie patch. Line it with 6.5-mm galvanised wire mesh and install a 1-m high mesh fence.

Whiteflies Use yellow sticky tape to monitor their population as well as trap them.

Aphids Back in Mrs Beeton's day, gardeners used a scissor-like tool with brushes instead of blades to remove these small green pests.

SNAILS AND SLUGS

Traps and lures These slimy pests are easy to catch but you do need to be vigilant, particularly if you have strappy plants, such as clivia, which provide great hiding places.

Beer bait Embed a shallow container in the garden and fill it with beer. Snails and slugs will crawl in and drown.

Ducks If your local government council regulations permit, and they can range freely, consider buying a few.

Crushing boots Walk around the garden at night or after rain, and stamp on any you find.

Flowerpot Turn it upside down and prop it up with a small rock so snails can use it as a haven. Check it each morning.

Length of pipe Hide it among some plants then check it every morning, removing any snails and slugs you find.

Copper tape When in contact with the metal tape, snail mucous creates an electrical charge.

Grapefruit Lure them with half a grapefruit.

HOMEMADE REMEDIES

Safe deterrent Use the following spray to repel these insects. Mix together ¼ cup liquid soap and ¼ litre vegetable oil. Store the spray in a labelled container in a cool place, and dilute it before spraying it onto your plants – 1 tablespoon concentrate to 1 litre water. Store this spray out of reach of children. Do not spray plants in hot weather as the spray can burn foliage.

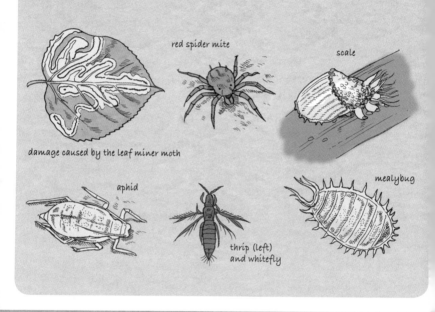

red spider mite

scale

damage caused by the leaf miner moth

aphid

thrip (left) and whitefly

mealybug

BENEFICIAL INSECTS

Nature's balance Learn to recognise these helpful creatures, and leave them to prey on insect pests.

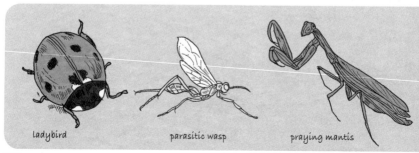

ladybird

parasitic wasp

praying mantis

ICK OFF BY HAND

ternal vigilance Sometimes the simplest methods are best – tour your garden every day, if you
an, and remove snails, slugs (see page 295) and other pests such as these.

cabbage white butterfly moth

green vegetable
bug

tomato hornworm

MAKING A FRUIT-FLY TRAP

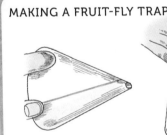

1 Make a paper funnel and
secure it with tape.

2 Put some banana skin
in a clean jar.

3 Insert the funnel in the jar so
fruit fly can fly in but can't get out.

And remember, if you spray your garden with chemicals, you will kill these as well.

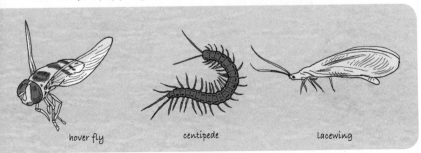

hover fly

centipede

lacewing

ATTRACTING WILDLIFE

Nature's helpers Another way to control pests is to entice wildlife, such as frogs, birds and lizards, into your garden. You also need to attract the pollinators, such as bees and butterflies, to help fertilise your plants.

8 USEFUL STRATEGIES

1 Plant fast-growing annuals such as sweet Alice (*Alyssym* sp.), which will attract beneficial insects. White-flowering plants attract night-flying insects.

2 Add a birdbath to attract birds, which will eat insect pests, and entice native birds into your garden by planting some native species.

3 Plant butterfly bush (*Buddleia* sp.), which will attract butterflies to your garden.

4 Provide rocks so skinks can bask in the sun, and hollow logs or pipes where they can hide.

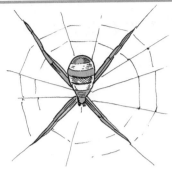

5 Consider adding a pond to your garden (see page 284) to attract frogs. Make sure there is a piece of wood or a rock against the side.

6 Leave spiders alone if you can – they'll catch and eat lots of pests, such as flies and mosquitoes.

7 Bees are essential for pollinating, especially if you have a produce garden. Plant lavender and other purple/violet flowering plants.

8 Red, pink (for example, camellia, above) and orange flowers (rhododendron) attract nectar-feeding birds.

MAKING BIRD FOOD

1 Combine 230 g suet, 260 g peanut butter, 320 g cornmeal and 180 g oats. Form balls.

2 Chill the balls in the fridge. Wrap each ball in a mesh bag and tie up with a piece of looped string.

3 Hang the ball from a branch that's out of reach of pets.

Companion Planting

Ancient practice This technique is based on centuries of observation by farmers and gardeners, who concluded that certain plants grow better together, or provide some other, less obvious benefits.

BENEFITS

Trap plants Sage will lure cabbage white butterflies away from brassica crops. Pick off the caterpillars before they become butterflies and lay eggs.

Nitrogen-fixing plants Return nitrogen to the soil by growing peas and beans. This benefits vegetables such as broccoli, cabbage and turnip.

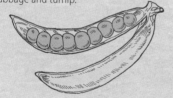

Barrier crops Protect vegetable crops with plants that exude a volatile oil. Aromatic herbs – for example, chives (above), lavender and rosemary – can confuse pests.

Nurse plants Farmers have traditionally grown raspberry canes under fruit trees, which provide shade for the berries.

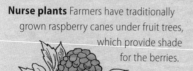

Beneficial plants Alfalfa, for example, helps break up compacted soils, retrieving nutrients from the subsoil.

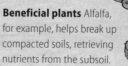

sweetcorn

beans

squash

The Three Sisters Native Americans have traditionally grown sweetcorn, climbing beans and squash together – the corn supports the beans, which return nitrogen to the soil, while the squash spreads over the ground, suppressing weeds. The vine's prickly hairs also deter pests while the beans and corn confuse the squash vine borer.

Weeds

Unwanted plants Instead of adopting a zero tolerance attitude to weeds, you could consider their benefits – some are edible, and any weed in your garden can be turned into a free liquid fertiliser.

EDIBLE WEEDS

Salad greens First make sure you have correctly identified the edible weeds in your garden, then try them to see which ones you like.

Purslane The new shoots of the succulent *Portulaca oleracea* are crisp.

Stinging nettle Add young shoots of *Urtica dioica* to cooked dishes but don't eat them raw, as the tiny hollow hairs contain chemicals that sting on contact.

Fat hen Also called lamb's quarters, *Chenopodium album* can be used in cooking. Try it as a basil substitute in pesto.

Chickweed *Stellaria media* can be eaten either fresh in salads or as a cooked vegetable.

Dandelion The young leaves of *Taraxacum officinale* can be eaten raw or sautéed, a process that reduces their bitterness.

Common amaranth The leaves of *Amaranthus retroflexus* are cut finely and used in an Indian dish, thoran.

WEED CONTROL

Smothering tactic Cover weed-filled beds with black plastic and they'll cook to death.

Chickens They help keep weeds under control by eating unwanted plants such as oxalis and chickweed (see opposite).

Mulch Suppress weeds with an organic mulch, such as sugarcane straw or compost.

Flowering weeds Remove weeds like oxalis before they flower and set seed.

Weeding tools To remove weeds with tap roots, such as the dandelion, use a special tool that looks like a flat fork.

FERTILISER

Weed tea Make use of weeds by piling them into an old rubbish bin and filling the bin with water. Replace the lid and leave it to break down for about 6 weeks. Then strain the weeds and use the tea diluted as a liquid fertiliser.

PROPAGATING

Free plants You can easily reproduce your favourite plants by using the appropriate propagation method. And if you're successful, you may enjoy giving away extra plants to friends and neighbours.

TAKING SOFTWOOD CUTTINGS

1 Fill a seed tray with free-draining compost, and firm it down. Cut stem tips.

2 Trim each stem to below a leaf joint, or node. Remove any leaves below that point.

3 Dip the stem into honey or rooting powder, then push it into the compost so that the lowest leaves are just above the surface, and water.

TAKING HARDWOOD CUTTINGS

1 If you have a large number of cuttings, prepare a trench with compost, then puncture it with a garden fork.

2 Take cuttings from healthy deciduous shrubs and trees in autumn and winter. Trim them into 25-cm lengths.

3 Push each cutting into the prepared holes until only the top third is above the surface.

AYERING

Choose a growing tip and bend it down to
il level. Mark the spot.

Dig a small hole that slopes at 45 degrees
n the side nearest the plant.

Make a wound in the stem, then plant it in
he hole. Peg into place and cover with soil.

TAKING ROOT CUTTINGS

1 Dig up the roots and wash
them thoroughly. Cut them
into sections, each about
5–8 cm long.

2 Make a flat cut at the top
and a slanting one at the
bottom of each cutting.

3 Push each section into
the potting mix until it is
level with the surface.
Cover it with grit.

TAKING LEAF CUTTINGS

1 With the leaf right side
down, use a sharp knife
to trim away the midrib.

2 If the leaf sections are
very long, cut them into
smaller sections.

3 Insert each piece, cut side
down, into the mix. Firm, water
and put in a warm place.

EXTENDING THE SEASON

Plant nurseries If you live in a cold climate, you may need to get a head start on planting for the growing season. Cold frames, greenhouses and cloches are all designed to protect tender young seedlings from the cold.

COLD FRAMES

Mini greenhouse Use a cold frame to start seedlings before the growing season. In a cold climate, it's worth building a permanent cold frame out of recycled materials.

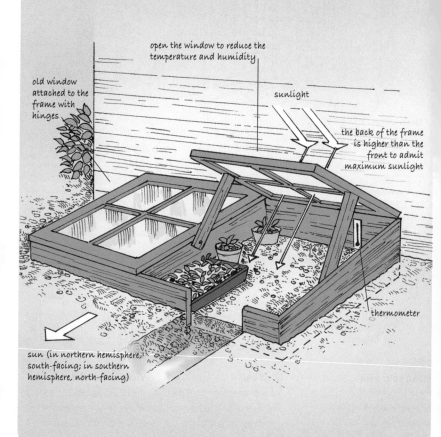

open the window to reduce the temperature and humidity

old window attached to the frame with hinges

sunlight

the back of the frame is higher than the front to admit maximum sunlight

thermometer

sun (in northern hemisphere, south-facing; in southern hemisphere, north-facing)

Orangeries Between the 17th and 19th centuries the owners of grand country estates in Britain and Europe constructed elaborate buildings to house their collections of citrus trees over winter. Huge windows admitted sunlight but excluded some of the cold; often a stove heated the orangery, helping citrus as well as other exotics to survive the cold months.

CLOCHES

Make your own Attach some metal hoops to a polystyrene box and cover them with a sheet of plastic.

Glass bell This cloche also protects seedlings from pests such as snails. Or use a plastic bottle (see page 45).

Victorian cloche Just turn the lid of this classic cloche whenever you need to let heat and humidity escape.

BULBS AND ANNUALS

Seasonal colour If you have the space, consider planting a stunning dri
of bluebells or daffodils, or pot up some hyacinth bulbs for indoor colour in
early spring. Use annuals in beds and containers to provide accents of colou

BULBS IN BULK

Mass-planting bulbs
Cast bulbs by the handful
over the area you wish to
plant, then remove plugs
of soil at the appropriate
depth before planting.

Propagating bulbs At planting
time, use a sharp knife to cut into the
basal plate at the bulb's base. Plant
the bulblets the next growing season.

BULB PLANTING GUIDE

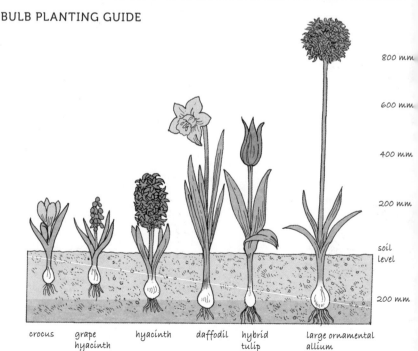

800 mm

600 mm

400 mm

200 mm

soil
level

200 mm

crocus   grape   hyacinth   daffodil   hybrid   large ornamental
          hyacinth   tulip   allium

LANTING SEEDLINGS

Once the true leaves appear fter the seed leaves), check or rootballs.

2 Place the seedlings in dappled shade for a week.

3 Move the tray to more direct light for another week.

Plant out the hardened-off eedlings on an overcast day.

5 Turn over the soil, and add compost if necessary.

6 Dig a hole for each seedling.

7 Gently remove each seedling from the tray, and plant at appropriate spacings.

8 Backfill the hole with soil, then add a thick layer of organic mulch.

9 Water daily until the seedlings become established.

Roses

The queen of flowers These garden beauties, which have inspired lovers, poets and playwrights throughout the ages, are remarkably hardy. Choose from shrub roses, ramblers, pillars and carpet types.

WHIP GRAFT

Propagation This technique works best when the scion is a similar size to the rootstock cutting. Start these in a greenhouse in midwinter, then graft in spring with semi-ripe shoots.

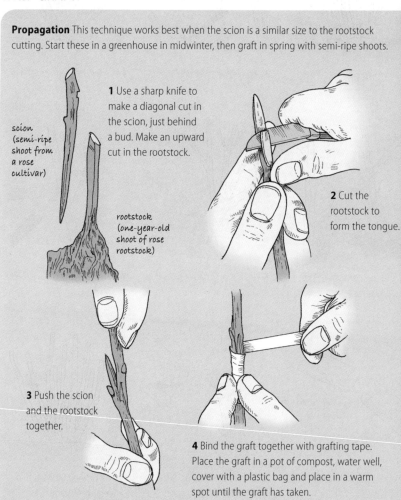

scion (semi-ripe shoot from a rose cultivar)

rootstock (one-year-old shoot of rose rootstock)

1 Use a sharp knife to make a diagonal cut in the scion, just behind a bud. Make an upward cut in the rootstock.

2 Cut the rootstock to form the tongue.

3 Push the scion and the rootstock together.

4 Bind the graft together with grafting tape. Place the graft in a pot of compost, water well, cover with a plastic bag and place in a warm spot until the graft has taken.

RUNING A ROSE BUSH

1 Cut brown or striated canes.

2 Remove pencil-thin canes.

3 Remove interior canes.

4 Prune off horizontal and crossed canes.

5 Pull out any suckers.

6 Cut above the outward-facing buds.

7 Prune back to healthy tissue.

8 Coat pruned stems with rose sealant.

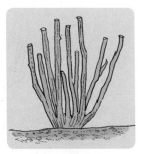

9 The pruned bush should have a vase shape.

LAWNS

Green carpet Lawns are not only water-guzzlers but also require a lot of maintenance, especially in summer, so it's worth considering reducing the area of grass. Grow a turf that suits your climate and soil type.

MOWING TIPS

Scythe Before lawnmowers were invented, lawns were cut by hand, using scythes, which required a sweeping action from one side to the other.

Sharp cuts Keep the blades sharp, as the cuts made by blunt blades will brown off.

Even ground Dips and rises can result in scalped areas, where the lawn is mown to bare earth. Try to level it.

Summertime In summer raise the blades a little and mow less often – taller grass helps retain moisture and shade the roots, and is less likely to become stressed in dry periods.

Dry grass Don't mow straight after rain as you won't be able to achieve an even effect.

Grass as mulch Rather than remove the clippings from the lawn, leave them to return moisture and nutrients to the soil.

LAWN TREATMENTS

Take care Don't end up with yellowing turf in a matt of dead grass and compacted soil.

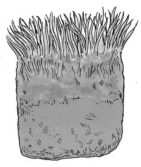

Weeding Remove deep-rooted weeds such as dandelion with a sharp knife or special tool (see page 303). Or add 1 cup salt to 4 litres white vinegar and use an old paintbrush to dab the solution on the weed only. In a few days it will die.

Dethatching Use a rake to remove the 'thatch' or layer of dead grass clippings.

Aerating Push a garden fork right down into the soil and move it back and forth. Work your way over the entire lawn.

FIXING A BARE PATCH

1 Use a garden fork to puncture the soil.

2 Scatter dry sand over the area, and rake it evenly.

3 Water in. The sand will improve the drainage.

LAWN ALTERNATIVES

Kidney weed Hardy and evergreen *Dichondra repens* spreads by runners.

Roman chamomile With delicate foliage, *Chamaemelum nobile* features daisy flowers.

Pennyroyal *Mentha pulegium* releases a menthol aroma when you walk on it.

NATURAL DISASTERS

Nature's fury Bushfires, earthquakes, hurricanes, cyclones, floods and blizzards – if your area is vulnerable to some form of natural disaster, take care to follow the guidelines provided by the appropriate authority.

BUSHFIRES

Prepare your home Nature is unpredictable. If you live in a bushfire area, do your best to guard against bushfires by following these guidelines. It may help save other people's lives as well as your own.

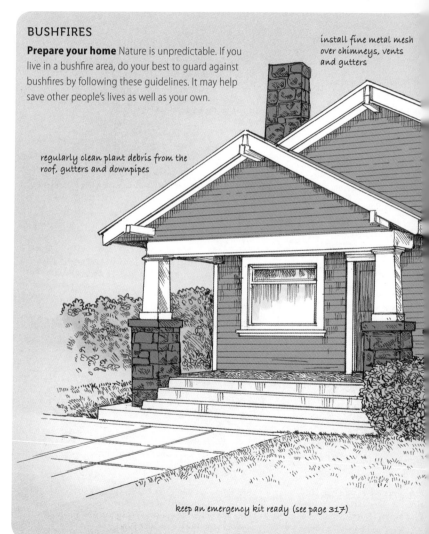

install fine metal mesh over chimneys, vents and gutters

regularly clean plant debris from the roof, gutters and downpipes

keep an emergency kit ready (see page 317)

do not plant trees so that they overhang the house; cut back any that do

plant trees and shrubs with a low oil content

cover the woodpile and keep it away from the house; do not hoard piles of dry prunings

keep grass mown and regularly clean up flammable plant debris, such as dry leaves

keep fire pumps and hoses (which should be long enough to reach the boundaries of the property) in good working order; and if you have a swimming pool or water tank, consider installing a portable pump

HURRICANE SAFETY TIPS

Batten down If you live in an area that is prone to severe storms, such as hurricanes and cyclones, check the local building regulations to make sure your home complies.

water mains tap

GENERAL TIPS

* Install window shutters or, when you're preparing for a storm, cover all windows with plywood.
* Stay away from windows.
* Identify the strongest part of your house in case you and your family need to take shelter there.
* Know how to turn off the power, gas and water, if necessary.
* Prepare an emergency kit (see the box opposite).

* Secure possible projectiles such as wheelie bins.
* If the eye of the storm is over your house, don't venture outdoors as the severe conditions will soon return.
* Empty the fridge and freezer, and leave the doors open.
* In case of lightning, do not use any electrical appliances or use the phone during the storm.
* Back up all computer files.

IN CASE OF A FLOOD

Evacuation plan Lock your home and take the recommended evacuation route. If you must enter floodwaters, wear sturdy boots but first check the water depth and current with a stick.

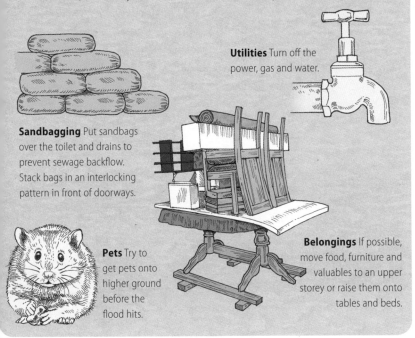

Utilities Turn off the power, gas and water.

Sandbagging Put sandbags over the toilet and drains to prevent sewage backflow. Stack bags in an interlocking pattern in front of doorways.

Pets Try to get pets onto higher ground before the flood hits.

Belongings If possible, move food, furniture and valuables to an upper storey or raise them onto tables and beds.

EMERGENCY KIT

* List of emergency phone numbers
* First aid kit (see page 356) – at least one member of the household should know how to administer first aid
* Portable radio (so you can listen to weather reports as well as emergency advice and warnings), torch, candles, matches and spare batteries
* Fresh water and non-perishables, such as tinned meat, fruit and vegetables
* Sturdy gloves and boots
* Warm clothing, personal mementos, valuables and mobile phones in strong waterproof bags
* Prescription medications
* Copies of essential documents, such as mortgage documents, insurance policies, passports and birth certificates, in sealable plastic bags
* Basic tool kit for emergency repairs
* Lightweight portable gas cooker in case of a long-term blackout

PETS

Whether your pet is a canary in a cage, a fish in a tank or a large (or small) furry member of the family, with the right food, exercise, attention and even affection, it will thrive in your care.

Popular dog breeds

Potential family member Before choosing a dog, consider your family and lifestyle, and how much time you'll have to spend with your pet. There's no point in having a Newfoundland in a tiny apartment.

Golden retriever An intelligent, easily trained, medium-sized dog, this breed is good with children. Gentle and charming, he loves to swim.

Pug This very affectionate small dog is great with children but he has a poor road sense and may be prone to certain health problems.

Beagle This hunting dog has a highly developed sense of smell, which can distract him. Gentle with children, he needs lots of exercise so he doesn't put on weight.

Miniature poodle Extremely intelligent and eager to please, the poodle can be trained by tone. He will thrive in a loving family but requires professional grooming for his coat.

Labrador retriever An excellent family dog, this athletic, lovable dog has webbed feet for swimming and also a great sense of hearing.

Bulldog The bulldog is a docile breed that has had aggression more or less bred out of him. He doesn't need as much exercise as other dogs.

Dachshund This small, outgoing and single-minded dog was bred to chase badgers down burrows. If hurt, he will defend himself, so think twice before choosing one as a companion to small children.

Cavalier King Charles spaniel A small companionable dog with an affectionate and obedient temperament, he needs regular grooming.

Out and about

Firm control Every time you take your dog for a walk you're likely to encounter curious children as well as other dogs and their owners, so you'll need to keep him on a leash and train him to obey you.

KEEPING TABS ON YOUR PET

Positive ID Many areas require dog and cat owners to register and microchip their pets.

1 The vet will implant a microchip so if your pet becomes lost, he can be scanned for his details.

2 Make sure your pet wears a collar and tag labelled with his name and a contact number.

3 Keep a photo of your pet in your wallet in case he becomes lost.

BE PREPARED

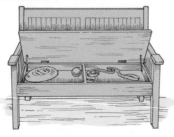
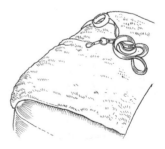

Going out Assign a drawer or bench storage (above left) to your dog so it's easy to pick up throwing toys and the leash as you leave the house for a walk. Protect the car seat with a rubber-backed bath mat that will stay in place (above right).

GREETING A STRANGE DOG

Cautious approach Never go up to a strange dog and attempt to pat him without first observing him and asking the owner's permission.

1 Ask the owner if it's OK first. Hold out your hand in a fist, palm down, so the dog can sniff it. Observe his reaction.

2 If the dog seems comfortable and reacts by loosely wagging its tail and sniffing your hand, it's OK to slowly and gently stroke him.

WALKING THE DOG

Obedience By nature dogs are pack animals. Demonstrate that you, the human, are the 'alpha dog' by walking ahead, with the short leash relaxed. If the dog strains ahead of you, it's asserting its dominance.

Leashes Don't use a retractable leash – if you need to get your dog out of trouble in a hurry, you may not be able to.

TRAINING DOGS AND CATS

A new pet As soon as you bring your dog or cat home, start training it. If it's still young, your task will be much easier but if you have rescued an abused animal from a shelter, you may need a lot of patience.

CAT IN THE HOUSE

Discipline To discourage your cat from unacceptable behaviour, clap your hands and use your tone of voice to express your disapproval.

Scratching post Encourage her to sharpen her claws on this instead of your sofa.

Protect wildlife Don't let your cat out at night, and make sure she wears a bell that will scare off birds.

Snug bed Make sure your kitten is warm and comfortable, and don't let her sleep on your bed, as she may fall off and injure herself.

A NEW PUPPY

Settling in Puppies need lots of attention and affection and firm, consistent training.

Walking Use a harness to take him out every few hours according to a timetable – he'll learn to poo and wee on walks.

Teething Provide your puppy with a chewing toy. Keep your shoes out of his reach, or sprinkle them with cloves.

Sleeping Buy a crate or kennel and a sleep pad, and get him used to sleeping in it. You can use a crate to take him to the vet, and he can use it as a refuge.

'PUPPY PROOFING' YOUR HOME

Remove temptation As you would with a toddler around the house, analyse your home for potential dangers. See also pages 352–5.

GENERAL TIPS

* Put dangerous chemicals out of his reach.
* Don't let blind cords and electric cords dangle, as he could strangle himself on the blind cord and electrocute himself on the other.
* Keep the lid of the toilet closed so he can't fall in and drown.
* Make sure he can't squeeze between the bars of the swimming pool fence or balcony railing, or run onto the road.

BODY LANGUAGE

Animal behaviour Learning to read your pet's body language may help you to interpret his or her mood.

relaxed – apparently asleep, with ears pricked

alert – tail straight and ears forward

bonding – cats rub their bodies against each other to exchange scents in a process called 'allorubbing'

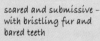

scared and submissive – with bristling fur and bared teeth

hunting – swishing tail, narrowed pupils and crouched posture

aggressive – twitching tail, raised hackles, flattened ears and bared teeth

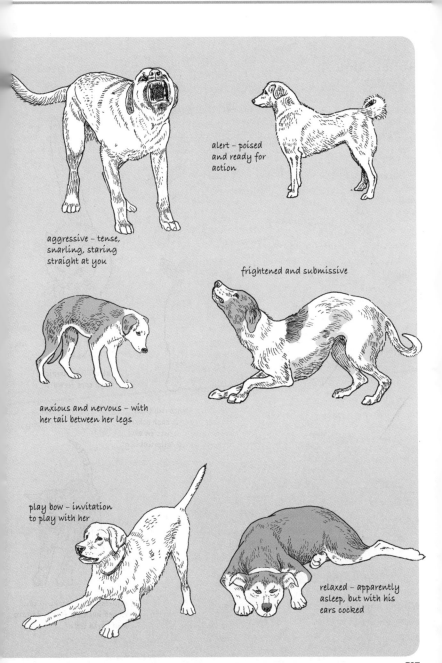

alert – poised and ready for action

aggressive – tense, snarling, staring straight at you

frightened and submissive

anxious and nervous – with her tail between her legs

play bow – invitation to play with her

relaxed – apparently asleep, but with his ears cocked

LIVING WITH CATS AND DOGS

Toilet etiquette Cats are naturally fastidious but you may still need to deter them from using your garden as a toilet. There's a clever, hygienic way to dispose of cat and dog excrement that won't add to landfill.

KEEPING CATS OUT OF THE VEGGIE PATCH

Deterrents Here are some strategies for discouraging your cat from fouling the veggie patch.

 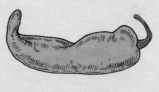 

'Scaredy cat plant' Grow a barrier of the herb *Plectranthus caninus*.

Cayenne pepper Sprinkle some of this spice, made from a red hot chilli.

Citrus peel Distribute orange, lime or lemon peel around the veggie patch.

TOILET TRAINING A KITTEN

Mother knows best If you have a kitten that is too young to have been house-trained by her mother, simply imitate her technique – place the kitten in the litter tray and scratch the litter with her own paws.

AN ELUSIVE CAT

The Cheshire cat Lewis Carroll's famous character from *Alice's Adventures in Wonderland* may have been inspired by the cheese moulds that used to be common in Cheshire, England.

MAKING A COMPOSTING PET TOILET

Out of sight All you need is an old plastic rubbish bin with a lid that clips on, and an out of the way spot in the garden, away from tree roots and the vegetable garden. Start by digging a hole that's at least big enough to accommodate the whole bin, but if you can, make it a bit deeper. Each time you add some poo, add some septic starter and some water.

 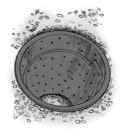 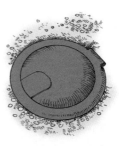

1 Drill holes all over the sides, then use a keyhole saw to remove the bottom. The holes will release the gases.

2 Fit the bin into the hole so that the lips sits snugly on the soil. Add some gravel and small rocks for drainage.

3 Replace the lid. If there is any danger of it being knocked off, weigh it down with a heavy stone or a couple of bricks.

CANINE HYGIENE

Territorial behaviour Take your dog outside regularly, otherwise he'll keep urinating in the same spot inside. If there's an accident, clean it up immediately and disinfect it. When out for a walk in the park, look for doggy bag bins (above left).

EXERCISE AND PLAY

Social life Like humans, all pets need exercise, play and attention for goo[d] health. Dogs in particular can become prone to problem behaviours such as digging and barking if they're neglected and unable to burn off energy.

RODENTS

Mice and rats They need plenty of exercise, such as that provided by a wheel, and also like ropes to climb and tubes to hide in.

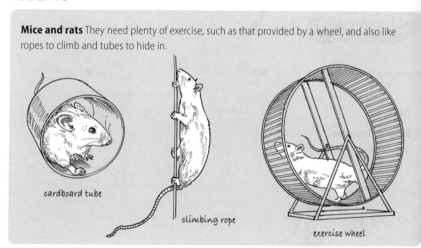

cardboard tube

climbing rope

exercise wheel

BIRDS

Dangling toys Birds love mirrors, bells and climbing toys.

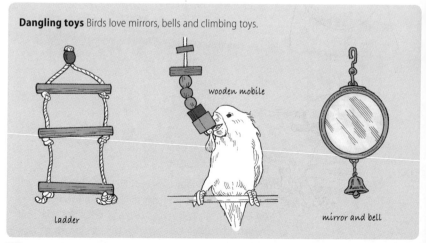

wooden mobile

ladder

mirror and bell

ATS

ommon household items Entertain your cat with items such as these but take care to keep all objects out of her reach so she can't choke on them.

paper bag or cardboard box   ball of scrunched up paper   a ball, or a ping-pong ball

DOGS

Simple pleasures Depending on the breed, most dogs need plenty of exercise and at least two walks a day.

an old soccer ball to chew on

a dog ball launcher keeps your hands free of dog saliva while the dog won't have to depend on your throwing skills

swimming is great exercise for dogs, and yours may also love retrieving sticks

CARING FOR CATS AND DOGS

Optimum health Ask your vet what sort of regular care your pet require at home. Neither cats nor dogs thrive on commercial pet food alone, and giving them fresh food to eat will result in fewer unpleasant odours!

GIVING YOUR CAT A PILL

 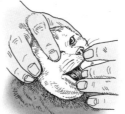 

1 Protect yourself from scratches by wrapping your cat in a towel.

2 With your hand on top of his head, press his jaw open.

3 Close his mouth and rub his chin until he swallows. Reward him with a treat.

CLIPPING YOUR CAT'S PAWS

1 When your cat is relaxed, hold his paw and press it gently to extend his claws.

2 Hold the clippers vertically as you cut.

3 Cut away from the quick at a 90 degree angle, then reward him with a treat.

DIET TIPS

chocolate is toxic to both cats and dogs

grate small amounts of fruit and vegetables into pet food

cooked bones may shatter and choke your pet

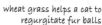

wheat grass helps a cat to regurgitate fur balls

BRUSHING YOUR DOG'S TEETH

1 When the dog is relaxed, let her sniff the special dog toothpaste.

2 With your hand above her head, lift her mouth open.

3 Hold her jaw firmly but gently, and brush her upper back teeth.

4 Brush her lower back teeth.

5 Check for signs of any problems, such as plaque build-up.

6 Reward your dog with praise and a treat.

RODENTS AND RABBITS

Engaging mammals A mouse, hamster or rabbit may be the ideal 'compromise' pet – something small and furry to please the children that will have less impact on your household than a dog or a cat.

MICE, RATS, HAMSTERS AND GUINEA PIGS

Mouse This curious creature can be trained to perform simple tasks. Keep two females for company (two males will become aggressive).

Rat You can train this intelligent, loyal pet to perform tricks. He should be well-socialised before he is sold to you, and needs at least an hour's interactive play per day.

Hamster Although he is colour-blind and near-sighted, this nocturnal mammal has a highly developed sense of smell and hearing. He stores food in pouches in his cheeks and eats his own faeces in order to digest food a second time.

Guinea pig A docile pet that enjoys being handled, he is most active at either end of the day. In the wild guinea pigs graze on grasses in small herds. Keep two or more for company. They communicate by vocalising.

HOLDING A RABBIT

The reluctant cuddler Rabbits don't like to be held as they prefer to be in contact with the ground where they can more easily detect predators and escape, if need be.

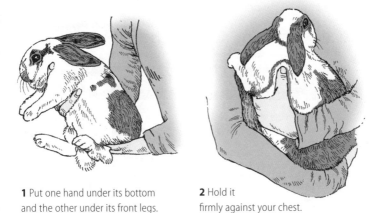

1 Put one hand under its bottom and the other under its front legs.

2 Hold it firmly against your chest.

THE BUNNY MANSION

Room to move The rabbit is a high-maintenance pet that needs plenty of time outside its cage. The hutch should be at last four times bigger than your rabbit.

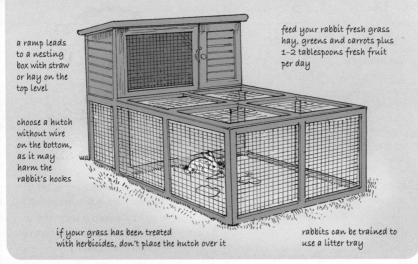

a ramp leads to a nesting box with straw or hay on the top level

feed your rabbit fresh grass hay, greens and carrots plus 1-2 tablespoons fresh fruit per day

choose a hutch without wire on the bottom, as it may harm the rabbit's hocks

if your grass has been treated with herbicides, don't place the hutch over it

rabbits can be trained to use a litter tray

AQUATIC PETS

Observation only Whether you enjoy watching beautiful tropical fish darting around an aquarium or prefer caring for amphibians, aquatic creatures make interesting pets.

THE AQUARIUM

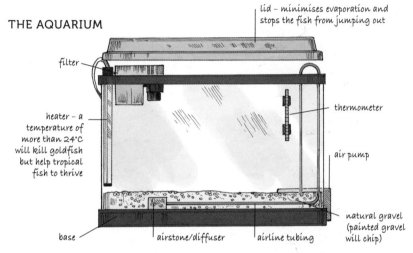

lid – minimises evaporation and stops the fish from jumping out

filter

heater – a temperature of more than 24°C will kill goldfish but help tropical fish to thrive

thermometer

air pump

base

airstone/diffuser

airline tubing

natural gravel (painted gravel will chip)

The basics You'll also need a fish net so you can remove sick or dead fish, an extra tank or bowl for quarantining sick fish, and some decorations, such as plastic plants (goldfish will eat real ones so you'll need to keep replacing those), small stones and holes for the fish to swim through.

CHANGING THE WATER

Maintenance Change at least 20 per cent of the aquarium water each week, but 50 per cent of the fishbowl water.

1 Let a clean bucket of tap water stand for 24 hours while the chlorine evaporates.

2 Use a length of tubing or a fish tank pump to remove the old water and debris. Rummage around in the gravel.

3 To prevent gravel blocking the hose, kink it with your hand. Once the new water is the same temperature as the old, carefully pour it in.

POPULAR AQUATIC PETS

Diverting hobby Children love unusual pets, such as the axolotl and turtle, while you may prefer to make a tropical aquarium a feature in your home.

Axolotl The larval stage of the salamander, it can live for up to 15 years without developing into an adult. It is sensitive to light, so position its tank away from direct light. It can grow up to 35 cm in length, so for one adult buy an aquarium that is at least 45 cm long.

Fish Goldfish (above left), a coldwater species that is easier to look after, can recognise individual humans and be trained to perform tricks. Tropical freshwater fish, such as the Regal angelfish (above right), are more demanding. Some tropical fish do best in schools while others are incompatible, so do your research and ask your supplier for advice.

Turtle A young turtle requires a 1-m long tank with temperature control and a piece of driftwood or a gravel beach so it can rest out of the water. This carnivore eats meat, worms and mosquito larvae. It needs access to sunlight 2–3 hours a week to keep it healthy.

BIRDS

Who's a pretty Polly? Do you want to interact with your bird, or just admire it? In general, the larger the bird, the more demanding it is, so it's a good idea to research the species you're interested in before purchasing.

BIRDS FOR NOVICE OWNERS

Finch This little bird sings lovely songs and does best in flight cages among a small flock. He doesn't like to be taken out and handled, so he's not appropriate for young children.

Budgerigar A type of parakeet, the budgerigar is entertaining and easy to train to perform tricks and talk. In a secure environment, let him out of his cage.

Lovebird If you're at work all day, keep two so they won't get lonely. They love to fly in front of a mirror over and over again. Very intelligent escapologists, they are also good mimics.

Canary Until 1987 male canaries were used in British mines to detect poisonous gas – they'd stop singing before they died. Install several perches at different heights so your canary can move around. These birds love water, so keep a big bowl in the cage.

HE BIRDCAGE

e right size Choose one that is large enough for your bird to spread his wings and flap, and
·sition it away from draughts and direct heat.

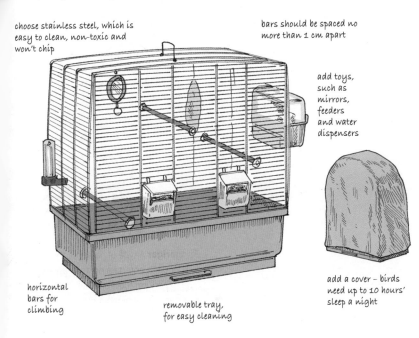

choose stainless steel, which is
easy to clean, non-toxic and
won't chip

bars should be spaced no
more than 1 cm apart

add toys,
such as
mirrors,
feeders
and water
dispensers

add a cover – birds
need up to 10 hours'
sleep a night

horizontal
bars for
climbing

removable tray,
for easy cleaning

GENERAL TIPS

Pine cone Give your
parrot a pine cone so
he can peck out the
seeds. It will also help
keep his beak trim.

Cleaning routine Change the cage
liner (don't use newsprint) and clean
the feeder and water container every
day, but clean out the whole cage
once a week.

Cuttlefish bone A
source of calcium, it
also helps your bird
to keep his beak trim.

KEEPING CHICKENS

Productive pets Chickens live for up to 10 years but the best layers are young, while they are still pullets, aged between 4 and 15 months. You'll need to worm your chickens every 3 months.

TRADITIONAL BREEDS

Good layers with easy temperaments Some people recommend cross-breeds that are reliable layers, while others say the best are traditional breeds. Here's a selection.

Black Australorp This is a sweet-tempered good layer of medium-sized brown eggs.

Rhode Island Red One of the best layers, the Rhode Island Red responds well to attention.

Silver-Laced Wyandottes This docile and handsome breed lays brown eggs.

Buff Orpington This calm breed lays large brown eggs.

Barred Plymouth Rock This cold-hardy breed is long-lived.

New Hampshire Keep this breed for eggs and meat.

ROOSTERS

Girls only Many areas ban roosters because of their pre-dawn crowing. Also, allowing your hens to lay fertilised eggs is more likely to make them broody and sit on them until they hatch.

CHICKEN FEED

Foragers If you're able to let your chickens wander around the garden, they'll eat pests and insects, grasses, clovers, weeds and herbs.

kitchen scraps | worms, snails, slugs and insects | weeds, grasses and herbs, such as comfrey (above)

HOUSING

Mobile home An A-frame kit coop, also called a tractor, will allow you to move the coop around the garden, spreading the wear on the grass. There should be a nesting box full of clean straw. When the veggie garden has gone to seed, let the chickens in, or move the coop over the beds so they can forage. Clean out the cage once a week.

SAFETY IN THE HOME

Avoid accidents in the home, especially those involving DIY enthusiasts and young children, by taking adequate precautions. Equip yourself with a first aid kit in case a mishap occurs.

ELECTRICAL SAFETY

Hands off! If a power tool or an appliance emits a spark, or acts strangely, turn it off straight away, unplug it and have it checked by a professional. And *never* touch electrical wiring yourself – again, hire a professional.

SOME GUIDELINES

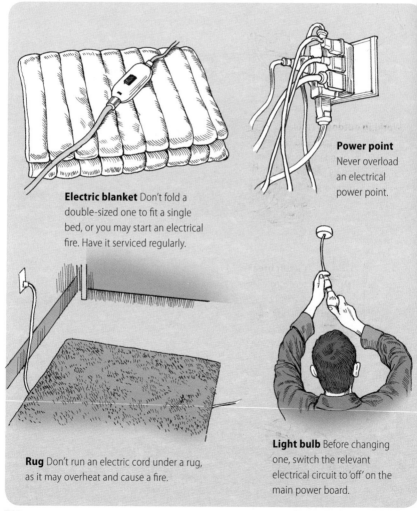

Electric blanket Don't fold a double-sized one to fit a single bed, or you may start an electrical fire. Have it serviced regularly.

Power point Never overload an electrical power point.

Rug Don't run an electric cord under a rug, as it may overheat and cause a fire.

Light bulb Before changing one, switch the relevant electrical circuit to 'off' on the main power board.

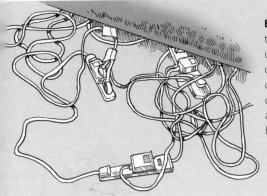

Extension cords Don't force them into small spaces or under furniture, where they can overheat. Check the capacity of each cord, and don't connect it to too many appliances at once. If a cord is hot to the touch, don't use it.

Working outdoors Ensure that both power tools and caravans are plugged into an earthed, safety switch-protected socket outlet.

Frayed cord Check power cords regularly, and have frayed or damaged ones fixed immediately.

Circuit breakers With these installed in your power box, the circuit will shut off as soon as it detects a problem.

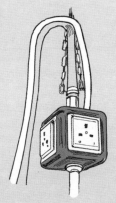

Workshop Keep the power point above the work area and cords out of the way of cutting tools.

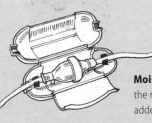

Moisture protection Never use a power tool in the rain, and use waterproofing accessories as an added safety measure against moist grass.

FIRE PROTECTION

Life-saving device Working smoke alarms can give you enough time to make a safe escape from a fire. Without them, however, the smoke can render you unconscious within a short time. See also 'Bushfires' on page 314.

ESCAPING A FIRE SAFELY

Fire drill Make sure the whole household knows what to do in an emergency. Agree on a meeting place outside the house, and ensure children know the emergency number for your area off by heart. Practise your fire drill regularly.

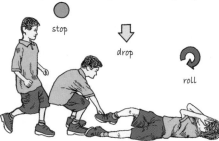

stop

drop

roll

Stop, drop and roll Teach children to extinguish flames on their clothes by suffocating them, and to keep low while escaping the house.

Escape route If it's not safe to escape through a window, touch the door of the room you're in. If it's hot to touch, don't open it. To block smoke, put a towel across the bottom of the door.

MAINTAINING SMOKE ALARMS

Essential precautions Fire services recommend you install long-life photoelectric-type smoke alarms, which need replacing every 10 years. Change a removable battery once a year or once it starts emitting a beep to indicate it is running low.

1 Test the alarm every month to make sure it's still working.

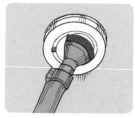

2 Twice a year, clean the alarm with the upholstery brush fitting on your vacuum cleaner.

3 Replace the removable battery once a year.

WHERE TO INSTALL SMOKE ALARMS

Safe coverage Install one in the living area – but not actually in the kitchen, as cooking will set it off all the time – and one in the hall, near bedrooms. Ideally, have one in each bedroom.

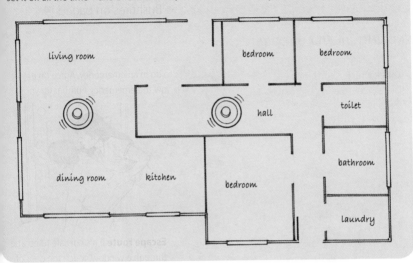

WHERE TO AVOID INSTALLING SMOKE ALARMS

Dead areas Don't install an alarm in the kitchen, bathroom or garage unless it is specially designed for these areas. Also avoid 'dead' areas – where smoke has difficulty reaching – and draughty spots.

Avoiding DIY accidents

Safe use Check the load rating of your ladder before using it, and make sure you set it up properly. Never over-reach – you should always have both feet on the same rung. If that's not possible, simply move the ladder.

SETTING UP A LADDER SAFELY

Quick check Stand facing the ladder with your feet touching its feet and your arms extended in front of you – if your palms can't rest on a rung at shoulder height, adjust the angle of the ladder.

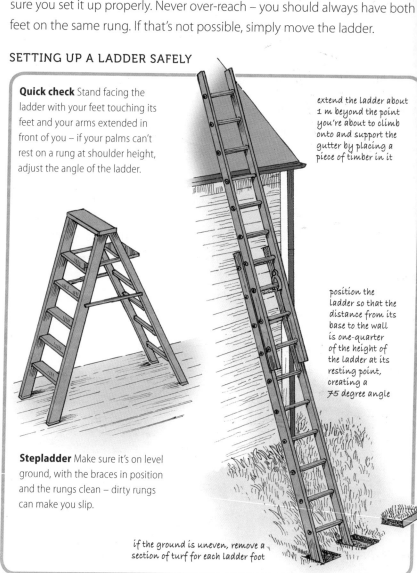

extend the ladder about 1 m beyond the point you're about to climb onto and support the gutter by placing a piece of timber in it

position the ladder so that the distance from its base to the wall is one-quarter of the height of the ladder at its resting point, creating a 75 degree angle

Stepladder Make sure it's on level ground, with the braces in position and the rungs clean – dirty rungs can make you slip.

if the ground is uneven, remove a section of turf for each ladder foot

USEFUL ADDITIONS

Ladder accessories These extras will not only make DIY jobs around the house easier but also reduce the risk of an accident occurring.

Ladder levellers Use these on steps.

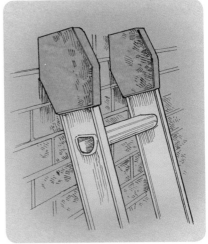

Pads Buy them, or make your own.

Stabiliser This accessory allows you to work at a practical distance from the wall.

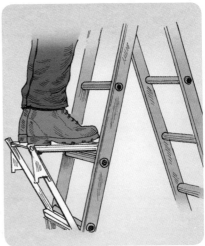

Work platform Designed for long periods standing on the ladder, it's ideal for painting.

HOUSEHOLD ACCIDENTS

Good sense Unfortunately, most accidents and injuries – from cuts and abrasions to burns and bad backs – occur in the home. Use this checklist to help you avoid common household accidents.

AVOIDANCE STRATEGIES

Predictable accidents Start training your children in basic home safety from an early age. A pair of pyjamas draped over a heater or an iron left unattended can have a tragic result.

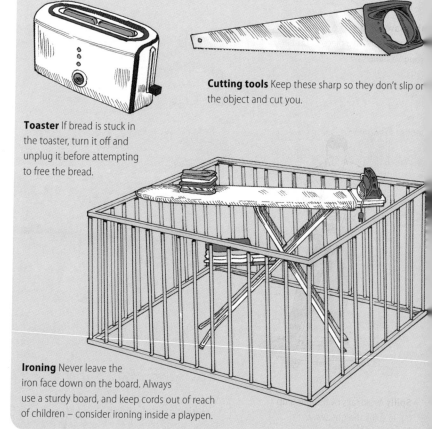

Cutting tools Keep these sharp so they don't slip or the object and cut you.

Toaster If bread is stuck in the toaster, turn it off and unplug it before attempting to free the bread.

Ironing Never leave the iron face down on the board. Always use a sturdy board, and keep cords out of reach of children – consider ironing inside a playpen.

Heaters Never drape clothes on heaters, and keep the clothes rack at a safe distance from them.

ble saw Always use a push stick or milar tool to push a piece of timber rough a table saw.

Lifting Store heavy items such as tool boxes on lower shelves – if you have to stretch to reach it, it's too high.

Spills Avoid falls by mopping up liquid spills straight away.

Safety glass Use laminated or toughened glass when replacing panes in windows and doors.

CHILDPROOFING YOUR HOM

A child's eye view The best way to anticipate disaster is to get down on your hands and knees and analyse your home from a small child's perspective. Remove potential dangers and take some simple precautions.

SAFETY GADGETS

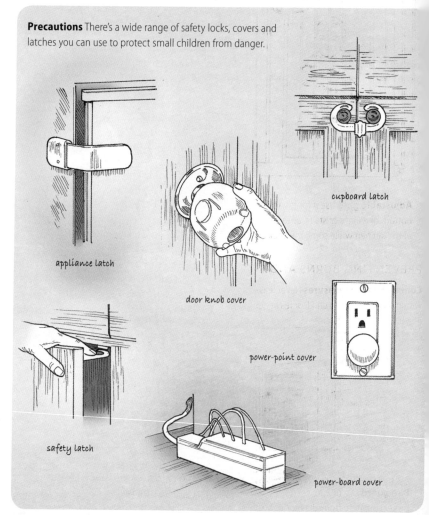

Precautions There's a wide range of safety locks, covers and latches you can use to protect small children from danger.

appliance latch

door knob cover

cupboard latch

power-point cover

safety latch

power-board cover

N THE MOVE

Containment Once your child is mobile, she will want to explore and you'll want to keep her safe.

Adjustable gate Use it for the top and bottom of a flight of stairs, or to keep baby out of the kitchen while someone cooks dinner.

Baby runner Dating back to at least the 17th century, this was once attached to a pole, secured to both the floor and a ceiling beam. The height was adjustable, and the toddler stood in the ring.

PREVENTING BURNS AND SCALDS

Common-sense measures Never leave a hot drink within reach of a small child, or leave her unsupervised in a bathroom or kitchen.

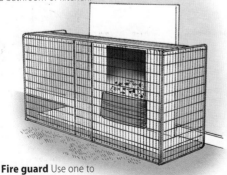

Fire guard Use one to protect children from all types of heating.

Stove Install a stove guard, and always keep the handles of pots and pans pointed inwards.

353

CLIMBERS

The intrepid explorer Most young children have a compulsion to explore, and some can't resist scaling furniture.

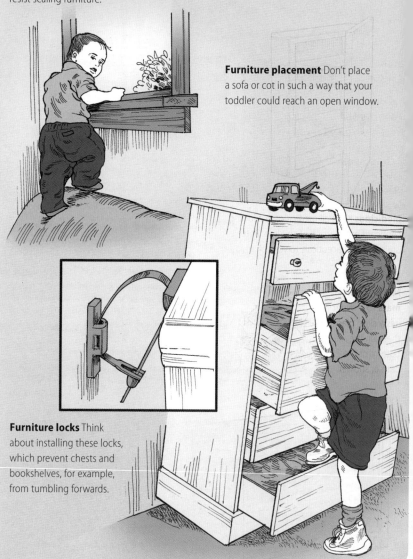

Furniture placement Don't place a sofa or cot in such a way that your toddler could reach an open window.

Furniture locks Think about installing these locks, which prevent chests and bookshelves, for example, from tumbling forwards.

PREVENTING ACCIDENTS

Think ahead These basic safety precautions will help avoid some common accidents.

Garden shed Make sure cleaning products, paints, pesticides and other poisonous chemicals are locked away in the shed or a secure cupboard.

Medicines Keep all medicines in a locked cupboard out of reach of children. Return unused pharmaceuticals to your pharmacist.

Mini suction mats To prevent nasty slips, place these on the bottom of the bath or shower.

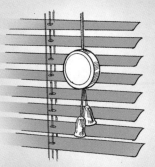

Blinds These blind cord windups prevent cords (a strangling risk) from dangling within reach of small children.

Toy box Timber storage boxes such as this one look attractive but there's a risk of the lid falling down and smashing little fingers. Consider using a lidless basket instead.

FIRST AID

Accidents do happen No matter how safety conscious and diligent you are, things can and do go wrong from time to time. If you are trained in first aid, you may help save a life.

FIRST AID KIT

Be prepared You can either buy a ready-made kit from your pharmacy or make your own. Store it in a waterproof container, and consider keeping a second one in your car.

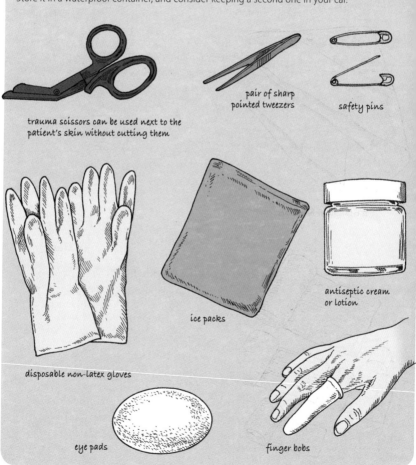

trauma scissors can be used next to the patient's skin without cutting them

pair of sharp pointed tweezers

safety pins

disposable non-latex gloves

ice packs

antiseptic cream or lotion

eye pads

finger bobs

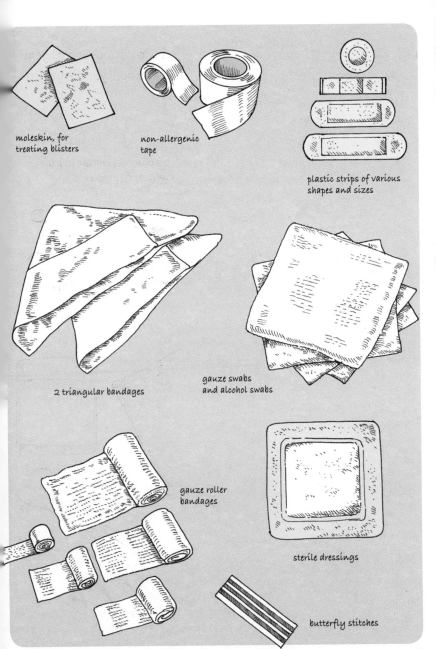

moleskin, for
treating blisters

non-allergenic
tape

plastic strips of various
shapes and sizes

2 triangular bandages

gauze swabs
and alcohol swabs

gauze roller
bandages

sterile dressings

butterfly stitches

TREATING HEAT EXHAUSTION

Cooling down Help the person to a shaded area, and ask him to lie down. Remove any extraneous items of clothing.

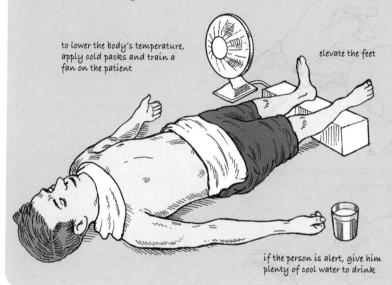

to lower the body's temperature, apply cold packs and train a fan on the patient

elevate the feet

if the person is alert, give him plenty of cool water to drink

TREATING A FIRST-DEGREE BURN

Burns and scalds These painful injuries are quite common, especially in the kitchen.

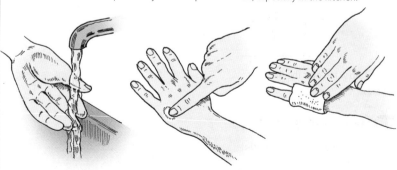

1 Run cool tap water over the site for about 20 minutes.

2 If the injury turns white, it's a first-degree burn.

3 Apply antibiotic ointment and a bandage.

TREATING SCALDS AND SERIOUS BURNS

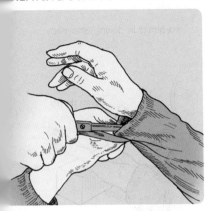

1 Remove clothing or jewellery, but not if it's sticking to the burn.

Immediate action Apply the same technique to chemical burns as for first-degree burns. Call an ambulance or take the patient to hospital.

CAUTION

* Don't apply butter, ointment or lotion to a burn, as it will help retain the heat.
* Don't touch the affected area.
* Don't burst any blisters.
* Don't try to remove anything that is sticking to a burn – leave it to medical staff.

2 Run cool tap water over the site for at least 20 minutes.

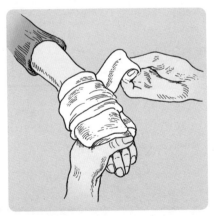

3 Protect the site with a sterile dressing, but apply it loosely.

TURN DOWN THE TEMPERATURE

* At 60°C, hot water causes third-degree burns in 1 second.
* At 55°C, hot water causes third-degree burns in 10 seconds.
* At 50°C, hot water causes third-degree burns in 5 minutes.
* The ideal temperature for bathing babies and young children is 37–38°C.

TREATING A BEE STING

Bee allergy If the person who has been stung is allergic to bee stings, she will go into anaphylactic shock, which is a medical emergency. See also the pressure immobilisation technique on page 363.

1 Remove the sting with a credit card or pair of tweezers.

2 Swab the site with some disinfectant.

3 Apply a paste of 1 part bicarbonate of soda and 1 part water, then an ice pack.

REMOVING A TICK

Serious consequences If you can't remove the tick yourself, or you are in an area where Lyme disease is a possibility, seek medical advice immediately.

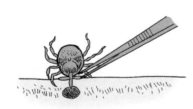 

GENERAL TIPS

* Use a pair of tweezers with fine, sharp points to remove the tick, placing them as close as possible to the tick's mouth. If you squeeze the tick's abdomen it may release more toxins.
* Don't try to swab the area with methylated spirits or petroleum jelly or the tick may release more toxins into your body.
* Don't twist the tick or you may remove the body and leave the head. Dispose of the tick without touching it.
* Clean the site with soap and water, then apply antihistamine cream.

REMOVING A SPLINTER

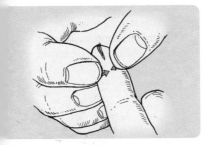

Wash the site and squeeze around the splinter.

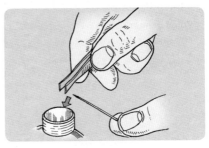

2 Disinfect a needle and a pair of tweezers.

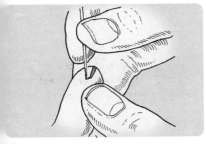

3 Enlarge the hole with the needle.

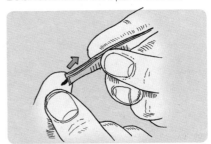

4 Remove the splinter.

REMOVING A SMALL OBJECT FROM THE EYE

Foreign object For large objects in the eye, always seek medical advice rather than attempt to remove it yourself. Place a clean pad on the injured eye, and close both eyes to keep the injured one from moving. For a small object, first wash your hands, then follow this sequence.

1 Try to remove the object with a clean cotton bud. Otherwise look down, and pull the lashes of the upper lid down over the lower.

2 If that fails, lie down, and flush the eye with a stream of sterile saline or tepid water.

3 Turn your head to the side to drain the excess liquid. If you are still unsuccessful, seek medical advice.

TREATING A VENOMOUS BITE

When danger strikes Even if you're lucky enough to live in an area where there are no native venomous spiders or snakes, you may still find yourself in a dangerous situation while travelling. First, call an ambulance, then apply first aid as follows. In some cases, you may have to perform CPR (see page 367).

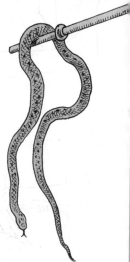

1 Reassure the patient, keeping her still to avoid spreading the venom.

2 Use a pressure immobilisation bandage (see opposite), which will apply firm pressure over both the bite and the affected limb.

3 If it is possible to do so safely, identify the culprit.

scorpions and spiders are both members of the arachnid family

PPLYING A PRESSURE IMMOBILISATION BANDAGE

eeping still If the patient has been bitten by a venomous spider or snake, call an ambulance, then eep the affected limb still so the venom doesn't circulate to the heart.

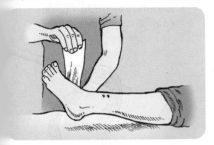

1 Use a broad pressure bandage to bandage the affected limb from below the bite site and up as far as possible.

2 Leave the toes free so you can check the circulation, and continue bandaging upwards from the site.

3 Bandage up the limb as far as you can, over the clothing.

4 Apply a splint. If you don't have enough bandages, use torn strips of clothing to secure it to the limb.

5 Continue to bind the splint.

6 If the bite is on a hand or arm, bandage the affected limb in the same way, but bend the elbow so the arm will be comfortable in a sling.

STOPPING A NOSE BLEED

1 Lean forwards while applying intermittent pressure to your nose.

2 Use a tissue or handkerchief to catch the blood.

3 Moisturise the lining of the nose. If bleeding persists, seek help.

STOPPING BLEEDING FROM A WOUND

When to call a doctor If the bleeding doesn't stop, or the person goes into shock, seek medical advice immediately.

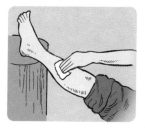 

1 Elevate the affected limb so it's above the heart, and apply firm pressure.

2 Use a pair of trauma scissors, if you have them, to cut away any constricting clothing.

 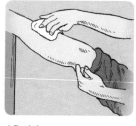

3 Cover the wound with a sterile dressing, and bandage.

4 Find the nearest pressure point (see the figure, right). Use it to slow the bleeding.

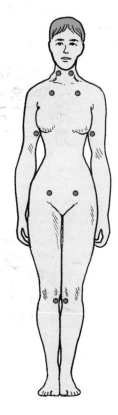

BANDAGING A WOUND

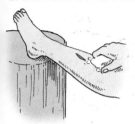 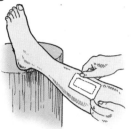 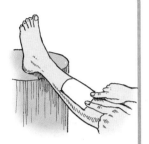

1 Elevate the affected limb and clean the site. Check to see if stitches are required.

2 Apply antibiotic ointment and cover with a bandage.

3 Apply a waterproof covering. If necessary, seek medical advice.

TYING A TOURNIQUET

Caution Only use a tourniquet when bleeding is severe. If the wound is just below a joint, knot above or close to the joint.

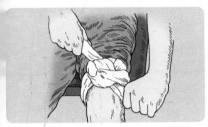 

1 Use a strong piece of non-stretch fabric to tie a knot above the injury.

2 Insert a stick into the knot.

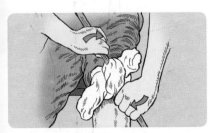 

3 Twist the stick, tightening the knot, until the bleeding stops.

4 Call the emergency number.

SAVING A CHOKING VICTIM

1 If the person is clearly choking, and unable to speak, call an ambulance.

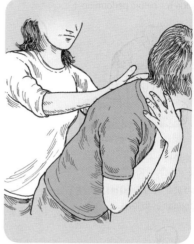

2 Strike the person's back 5 times.

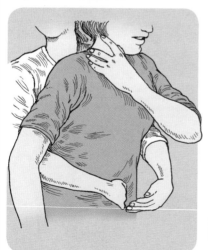

3 Place your fist below the patient's ribs.

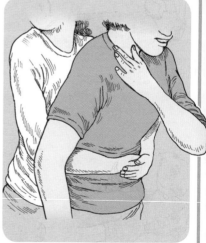

4 Place your other hand flat over your fist and give 5 abdominal thrusts.

PERFORMING CPR ON AN ADULT

Training First aid agencies recommend you have training in this technique – for adults, not children – before performing it.

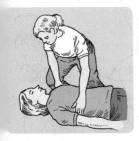

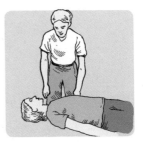

1 Ask the person if they are OK. If there is no response, and you are trained in CPR, continue as follows.

2 Listen for signs of breathing.

3 Briefly feel for a pulse. If the person has stopped breathing and there is no pulse, call an ambulance and start CPR.

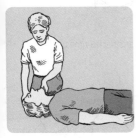

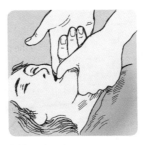

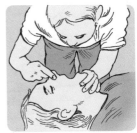

4 Tilt back the chin.

5 Clear the airway.

6 Pinch the nostrils.

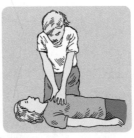

7 Blow into her mouth with 2 one-second breaths.

8 Pump on the breastbone 30 times.

9 Repeat steps 6–8 until medical assistance arrives.

WRAPPING A SLING

1 Place the fabric, folded in a triangle, over your shoulder and under your arm.

2 Bring the bottom point of the triangle over your other shoulder.

3 If you're alone, ask someone else to knot the sling at the back of your neck. Otherwise, knot it before you slip it over your shoulder.

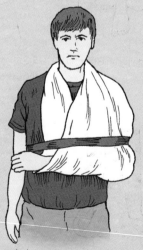

4 Use a belt or rope to secure your arm and prevent further movement until you can receive medical treatment.

PLINTING A LOWER LEG INJURY

1 Remove the shoe and sock, and call an ambulance.

2 Position a folded mat under the injured limb.

3 For extra support of the limb, place some padding behind the knee.

4 Add padding on either side of the leg.

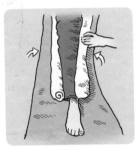

5 Gather the padding around the leg.

6 At intervals use string to tie the padding around the leg.

7 Fold up the bottom of the mat and pull the rope through the fold.

8 Roll up the excess padding.

9 Crisscross and tie off.

CONVERSION TABLES

When you're cooking from a recipe that doesn't give metric or imperial equivalents, use these handy conversion tables for spoons and cups, temperature, weight and volume.

CONVERSION TABLES

CUP CONVERSIONS

Ingredients	Cup	Metric	Imperial
Almond meal	1	110 g	4 oz
Almonds, whole	1	160 g	5½ oz
Beans, dried	1	200 g	7 oz
Breadcrumbs, commercial	1	110 g	4 oz
Butter, margarine	1	250 g	9 oz
Cheese, parmesan (grated)	1	100 g	3½ oz
Chocolate, grated	1	100 g	3½ oz
Cocoa powder	1	110 g	4 oz
Coconut, desiccated	1	75 g	2½ oz
Coriander, fresh	1	40 g	1½ oz
Flour, white	1	125 g	4½ oz
Ginger, chopped	1	100 g	3½ oz
Honey	1	340 g	12 oz
Jams, jellies	1	320 g	11 oz
Lentils	1	200 g	7 oz
Mascarpone	1	250 g	9 oz
Mint, fresh	1	35 g	1¼ oz
Parsley, fresh	1	40 g	1½ oz
Peanuts, whole	1	150 g	5¼ oz
Polenta	1	170 g	6 oz

Ingredients	Cup	Metric	Imperial
Potato, mashed	1	225 g	8 oz
Rice, arborio	1	220 g	7½ oz
Rice, brown	1	200 g	7 oz
Rice, long-grain (cooked)	1	185 g	6½ oz
Rice, long-grain (uncooked)	1	200 g	7 oz
Rolled oats	1	100 g	3½ oz
Semolina	1	160 g	5½ oz
Sour cream	1	250 g	9 oz
Sugar, brown	1	200 g	7 oz
Sugar, caster	1	225 g	8 oz
Sugar, demerara	1	250 g	9 oz
Sugar, white	1	220 g	7½ oz
Sugar, raw	1	250 g	9 oz
Sultanas and raisins	1	225 g	8 oz
Tomato paste	1	250 g	9 oz
Tomatoes, chopped	1	200 g	7 oz
Vegetable oil	1	220 g	7½ oz
Walnuts, chopped	1	120 g	4¼ oz
Yogurt, natural	1	250 g	9 oz

CONVERSION TABLES

OVEN TEMPERATURE CONVERSIONS

Farenheit	Centigrade	Gas Mark	Description
225°F	105°C	¼	Very cool/slow
250°F	120°C	½	Very cool/slow
275°F	135°C	1	Cool
300°F	150°C	2	Cool
325°F	165°C	3	Very moderate
350°F	180°C	4	Moderate
375°F	190°C	5	Moderate
400°F	200°C	6	Moderately hot
425°F	220°C	7	Hot
450°F	230°C	8	Very hot
475°F	245°C	9	Very hot

SPOON AND CUP CONVERSIONS

Quantity	Australia	Britain	United States
1 cup	250 ml	284 ml	237 ml
¾ cup	180 ml	213 ml	178 ml
⅔ cup	160 ml	190 ml	158 ml
½ cup	125 ml	142 ml	119 ml
⅓ cup	80 ml	95 ml	79 ml
¼ cup	60 ml	71 ml	59 ml
1 tablespoon	20 ml	15 ml	15ml
1 teaspoon	5 ml	5 ml	5 ml

WEIGHT CONVERSIONS

Metric	Imperial	Metric	Imperial
10 g	⅓ oz	250 g	9 oz
50 g	2 oz	375 g	13 oz
80 g	3 oz	500 g	1 lb
100 g	3½ oz	750 g	1 lb 9 oz
150 g	5 oz	1 kg	2 lb 2 oz
175 g	6 oz	1.5 kg	3 lb 5 oz

VOLUME CONVERSIONS

Metric	Imperial (Brit.)	Imperial (US)
20 ml	½ fl oz	½ fl oz
60 ml	2 fl oz	2 fl oz
80 ml	3 fl oz	3 fl oz
125 ml	4½ fl oz	4 fl oz
160 ml	5½ fl oz	5½ fl oz
180 ml	6 fl oz	6 fl oz
250 ml	9 fl oz	8½ fl oz
375 ml	13 fl oz	13 fl oz
500 ml	18 fl oz	17 fl oz
750 ml	26 fl oz	25 fl oz
1 litre	35 fl oz	34 fl oz

INDEX

WeldonOwen
PUBLISHING

Published by
WeldonOwen Publishing
Ground Floor 42–44 Victoria Street, McMahons Point
Sydney NSW 2060, Australia
weldonowenpublishing.com

Copyright © 2012 Weldon Owen Pty Ltd

Managing Director Kay Scarlett
Publisher Corinne Roberts
Creative Director Sue Burk
Senior Vice President, International Sales Stuart Laurence
Sales Manager, North America Ellen Towell
Administration Manager, International Sales Kristine Ravn

Managing Editor Averil Moffat
Project Editor Sarah Baker
Designer transformer creative
Images Manager Trucie Henderson
Editorial Assistance Shan Wolody
Production Director Todd Rechner
Production and Prepress Controller Mike Crowton
Illustrations Peter Bull Art Studio

ISBN 978-1-74252-283-8

Printed and bound in China by Hang Tai Printing Company Limited.

The paper used in the manufacture of this book is sourced from wood
grown in sustainable forests. It complies with the
Environmental Management System Standard ISO 14001:2004

Disclaimer Before carrying out even the simplest DIY tasks around the home, such as dismantling the trap on the kitchen sink, check that it is legal for you to do so. While every effort has been taken to ensure that the information in this book is accurate, the publisher does not guarantee, and accepts no legal liability whatsoever arising from or connected to, the accuracy, reliability, currency or completeness of any material contained in this book.